Archangel Raphael

Connecting with the Angel of Healing

© Copyright 2024 - All rights reserved.

The content contained within this book may not be reproduced, duplicated, or transmitted without direct written permission from the author or the publisher.

Under no circumstances will any blame or legal responsibility be held against the publisher, or author, for any damages, reparation, or monetary loss due to the information contained within this book, either directly or indirectly.

Legal Notice:

This book is copyright protected. It is only for personal use. You cannot amend, distribute, sell, use, quote, or paraphrase any of the content within this book without the consent of the author or publisher.

Disclaimer Notice:

Please note the information contained within this document is for educational and entertainment purposes only. All effort has been executed to present accurate, up-to-date, reliable, and complete information. No warranties of any kind are declared or implied. Readers acknowledge that the author is not engaging in the rendering of legal, financial, medical, or professional advice. The content within this book has been derived from various sources. Please consult a licensed professional before attempting any techniques outlined in this book.

By reading this document, the reader agrees that under no circumstances is the author responsible for any losses, direct or indirect, that are incurred as a result of the use of the information contained within this document, including, but not limited to, errors, omissions, or inaccuracies.

Your Free Gift
(only available for a limited time)

Thanks for getting this book! If you want to learn more about various spirituality topics, then join Mari Silva's community and get a free guided meditation MP3 for awakening your third eye. This guided meditation mp3 is designed to open and strengthen ones third eye so you can experience a higher state of consciousness. Simply visit the link below the image to get started.

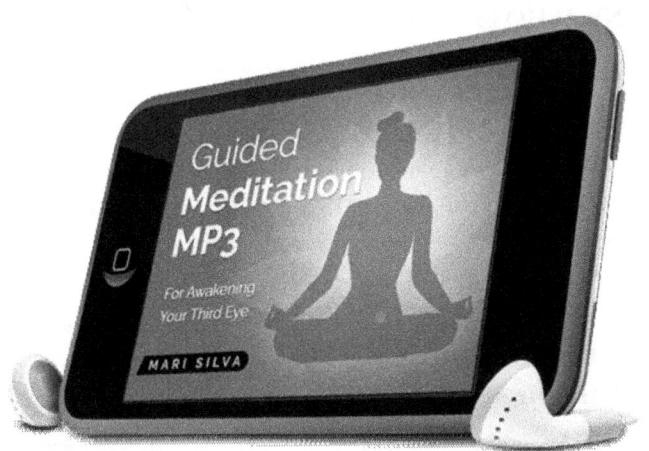

https://spiritualityspot.com/meditation

Table of Contents

INTRODUCTION 1
CHAPTER ONE: WHO IS ARCHANGEL RAPHAEL? 3
CHAPTER TWO: WHEN AND HOW TO CALL UPON ARCHANGEL RAPHAEL 12
CHAPTER THREE: SIGNS THAT ARCHANGEL RAPHAEL IS PRESENT 24
CHAPTER FOUR: HEALING NEGATIVE THOUGHTS AND EMOTIONS 32
CHAPTER FIVE: HEALING RELATIONSHIPS AND MARRIAGES 43
CHAPTER SIX: HEALING THE PHYSICAL BODY 53
CHAPTER SEVEN: ANGELIC REIKI 63
CHAPTER EIGHT: HEALING FOR HEALERS 75
CHAPTER NINE: CREATIVE RITUALS 82
CONCLUSION 90
CORRESPONDENCES SHEET 92
HERE'S ANOTHER BOOK BY MARI SILVA THAT YOU MIGHT LIKE 94
YOUR FREE GIFT (ONLY AVAILABLE FOR A LIMITED TIME) 95
REFERENCES 96

Introduction

There is more to this world than meets the eye. And if you've ever wondered how you can tap into this "more," you will discover that there is no better way than to do so with the help of a celestial being. *But not just any celestial being.* This book is about Archangel Raphael, the Healer of all healers who brings you loving relationships and infinite creativity.

Within these next pages, you will discover the mystical world of Raphael. You will learn that you have barely scratched the surface of how good things can get for you regarding your health, relationships, and creativity.

As you go through each page and chapter, you will learn all about the power you have not taken advantage of until this point in your life. The veil of the celestial world will start to lift, and you will discover all the blessings that have been waiting for you, accessible through a relationship with Archangel Raphael.

Unlike other books on this topic, you will find this one very easy to read and digest. Whether you're a beginner at working with celestial beings or have been working with others other than Raphael, you will find everything you need in this book. It is packed with hands-on instructions and methods broken down step by step so that you never feel lost at any point when connecting with Archangel Raphael.

Are you ready to let Raphael lead you through the depths of your imagination and subconscious to the life you've always wanted regarding health, relationships, and inspiration? This book is definitely the one for you. So, if you are ready to have your life transformed by the emerald green light of Raphael, go ahead and dive into the first chapter.

Chapter One: Who Is Archangel Raphael?

Who Is Raphael?

Archangel Raphael is known as the Medicine of God. According to the Zohar, this Archangel has one chief task: To heal humanity and the earth itself. "Raphael" means "God heals" or "God has healed," and he's also referred to as the "divine physician" and everyone's guardian angel. Whether your problems are spiritual, mental, physical, or emotional, you can trust Raphael to heal you. This Archangel became known to humanity through the Book of Tobit and the first book of Enoch. Many old and new stories talk about this Archangel's healing powers. After the "father of all nations," Abraham, was circumcised, Archangel Raphael healed him. When Jacob dislocated his hip after wrestling with an angel, Raphael put it back into place.

A depiction of Archangel Raphael.
https://pixabay.com/es/illustrations/arc%C3%A1ngel-rafael-arc%C3%A1ngel-angel-7964678/

Raphael, According to Tobit

Tobit was known as a righteous and trustworthy man. Everyone agreed that he always did the right thing. He was devoted to God and did his best to offer others help when he could. He was married to Anna, and they had Tobias, their son. Tobit never strayed from his belief in God. However, that would soon be the reason behind his downfall. For many, his goodness was just too good to be true. Tobit was getting death threats, and on top of that, everything he had was taken from him. That was around the time when most Jews had been captured and being held in Nineveh. The evil King Sennacherib staunchly refused to allow them to pay their respects to those they'd lost and bury them properly. Not many people could stand up to Sennacherib's callousness, but Tobit was one of those who did. He did his best to secretly bury the dead.

One evening, when Tobit was about to have dinner, he was informed of a body that had to be buried. At this point, the man was *fifty*. Regardless, he sprung up and went to help.

According to tradition, handling a dead body meant being defiled, so he couldn't return to his meal. Instead, he spent the night outside his courtyard, sleeping by the wall, where some sparrows were perched; little did he know that this would lead to disaster. While he slept, his face was exposed, and bird droppings got into his eyes. When he woke up, he was blind. No matter who he saw about the condition, no one could cure him. Being blind meant he could no longer make money, and Anna was forced to provide for the family.

With time, Tobit's condition caused him so much shame and feelings of sadness. After eight years, he was so tired of living that way that he prayed for death. Around the same time, someone else was praying for the very same thing. The other prayer was from Raguel's daughter Sara, who had been widowed seven times because Asmodeus the demon kept killing her husband before they could consummate their marriage. God decided to show mercy by sending Raphael to answer Sara's and Tobit's prayers.

As Tobit spent his time waiting for death, he worked to ensure everything was in order before it happened. He had Tobias go to Media for money that a business associate, Gabriel, owed him. That was a dangerous trip, so he instructed Tobias to travel with someone to keep him safe, promising to pay them for their trouble. His traveling companion would be Azarias, a distant relative. Tobias didn't know that Azarias was actually Raphael disguising himself as human. Tobit had no clue, either. He simply wished his son well and sent him on his way.

On the first night of their trip, Tobias and Azarias stopped by the Tigris River to make camp. It was a long trip, so Tobias went to wash in the river, and as he did, he saw a huge fish. Raphael asked Tobias to catch the fish and remove its gallbladder, liver, and heart. They cooked the fish for dinner, and as they ate, Tobias wondered what his travel companion needed the fish's organs for. Azarias claimed that with the liver and heart, he could create smoke that would drive away evil spirits, and the gallbladder could help the blind see again.

They continued the next day, and as they drew closer to their destination, Azarias told Tobias it would be best to stay at Raguel's house. He also suggested that Tobias marry Sara. But of course, he couldn't hide the fact that the woman was thought to bring horrible luck to any man she married. When Tobias learned about her past, he panicked. But Azarias told him it would be fine if he just put the fish liver and heart on an incense burner and let the "lovely" scent send the demon that plagued Sara away. And he was right. When Asmodeus, the husband killer, smelled the incense, it was so rank that he ran and didn't stop until he reached the Northern part of Egypt! As Raphael, Azarias chased after him and bound him so he couldn't cause any more trouble. The next day, Tobias had come out of the bridal chamber alive and kicking – a shock to Sara's dad, Raguel, who had been hard at work the night before, digging what he thought would be Tobias's grave.

For the next 14 days, there was constant celebration. After that, Tobias returned home with his new bride and his strange friend, Azarias, by his side. Azarias had mentioned that fish gallbladder could heal the blind, so Anna told her son to anoint Tobit's eyes with the foul-smelling organ. Tobit's eyes prickled and then teared up, forcing him to rub them hard. As he did, the white film fell off, and he could see again. This was yet another reason to celebrate, and the family thanked Azarias profusely, giving him half of the ten silver talents they brought back from Media.

At this point, Azarias announced his true identity, making Tobias and Tobit quake in their boots! Were they in the presence of an actual Archangel the whole time? They were so scared that they fell to the floor. Raphael comforted them, saying there was no need to be scared. He told them to keep being good men and journal everything they'd experienced. Tobit lived another hundred years before passing away. As for his son Tobias and his daughter-in-law, Sara, they would go on to have six sons and enjoy a beautiful life together, all thanks to Raphael, who continues his healing work to this day.

Raphael, According to Enoch

Raphael appears several times in the Book of Enoch. The Archangels, Michael, Sariel, and Raphael, were watching the Watchers, also called the sons of God in the book of Job, Chapter 1, verse 6. The Watchers were the Nephilim, giants of old who were sons of angels and humans, under the leadership of As'a'el and Semhazah. The giants taught humans about jewelry, cosmetics, war, weapons, astrology, and magic spells – things ruining humanity. So, God asked the Archangels to go and punish them.

Raphael's instructions from God, as recorded in the book of Enoch, Chapter 10, verses 4 to 5, were to "Bind As'a'el; fetter him hand and foot and cast him into darkness; make an opening in the desert... and cast him in. And place upon him jagged and rough rocks, and cover him with darkness and let him abide there for all time, and cover his face that he may not see the light." As you can probably tell, God had had enough of As'a'el. The other Watchers were apprehended by Michael and placed in underground prisons to remain there for seventy generations. At the same time, Gabriel set up the Nephilim to battle each other until they were all dead.

Raphael also interacted with famous Bible characters like Noah and King Solomon. It was Raphael who helped make Noah's ark. Jewish records also say that after the flood had abated, Raphael gave Noah a book of medicine called the Sefer Raziel, which belonged to Angel Raziel. The book mostly had spells but is sadly now lost. As for the great King Solomon, Raphael helped him construct the Great Temple when he faced challenges and prayed to God for assistance. So, God sent the Archangel to Solomon. He went bearing a special ring on which a pentagram was engraved. This ring remains vital in magic, even today, and it's why some refer to Raphael as the angel of magic and miracles. It's also worth noting that the pentagram is an ancient medical symbol. With this ring, Solomon summoned and commanded thousands of demons to serve as laborers and finish the temple's construction.

Raphael in Islam

Also called Israfil, Esraful, or Israfel, this Archangel is highly esteemed in Islam. He's the one who will blow the trumpet of judgment, which he continues to keep close to his lips, awaiting God's instruction. He was created at the dawn of time with four wings and incredible height that let him reach heaven's pillars from Earth. He is also a musical angel who sings songs of praise to God in a thousand languages. He is the go-between for God and the other angels, passing along God's instructions to the hosts of angels. Some insist he had been in touch with the prophet Muhammad even before the encounter with Gabriel.

The Sufi believe in the perfect human, known as the Qutb. This person is said to be similar to Israfil, as they have a heart like his. According to Ath-Tha'labi's narration of Islamic tradition, Rafa'il and Dhu al-Qarnayn (whom some call Alexander the Great) met. The Archangel spoke about the Water of Life or Ayn al-Hayat, and this made Dhu al-Qarnayn crave it, but Khidr, his cousin, was the one who got to drink it.

Raphael in Other Texts

In the Testament of Solomon - a part of the Pseudepigrapha - a demon afflicted a young boy by sucking on his thumb, which made him feel weak and lose weight. To help the boy, Solomon prayed, and Michael was sent as an answer. Michael had a ring meant to capture evil spirits, but this isn't the same as the ring Raphael offered Solomon for the temple's construction. With this ring, Solomon captured Ornias, the spirit plaguing the boy. He grilled Ornias with questions until the demon was forced to summon Beelzebub, who was immediately bound by the ring. After much persuasion, Beelzebub brought every demon to Solomon to quiz all of them. He learned their names, powers, all they knew about astrology and the powerful angels they couldn't stand a chance against. One of the demons was Oropel, who gave people nasty sore throats, but would take off in fright whenever he heard Raphael's name.

The healing effect of Bethesda's pond is Raphael at work. In the Gospel of John, Chapter 5, verses 2 to 4, many people gathered around it with different ailments or ailing relatives and friends, waiting for it to begin moving. The movement was caused by an angel getting into the pond. The first person to get into the water after the angel would be healed of whatever was wrong with them.

In Milton's Paradise Lost, Adam and Eve are warned by Raphael not to defy God's word. He was kind and loving in his delivery. Raphael spoke with Adam at length on all kinds of things. In the end, Raphael warned Adam to be mindful of his interactions with the tempter, Satan, and not to touch the forbidden fruit. Of course, you know how that story played out.

Raphael was one of the angels Abraham conversed with in the Talmud at the oak of Mamre in Hebron. Michael was in the middle, while Gabriel and Raphael were to his left and right, respectively. They all had specific tasks to handle. Gabriel would destroy Sodom, Michael would let Sarah know she'd become the mother to Isaac, and Raphael would help Abraham heal after his circumcision and come to Lot's rescue, too.

According to the Midrash Konen, Raphael was Libbiel once upon a time. Libbiel is Hebrew for "God is my heart." According to this text, before the creation of man, God met with his angels about it. Not all the angels were okay with God's decision. The angels of justice and love okayed God's decision. Still, the angels of peace and truth worried that humans would become dishonest and problematic. In response, God cast the angel of truth to the Earth. Naturally, this upset the other angels, but God responded by telling them, "Truth will spring back out of the earth."

Interestingly, even before the angels voiced their concerns, God only shared the good things about humanity, not the uglier side. The dissenting angels asked, "What is man, that Thou art mindful of him? And the son of man, that Thou visiteth him?"

God responded that all the other creations would be pointless without anyone to appreciate and enjoy them. Some angels went along with God's plan. In contrast, others continued to oppose him, which meant they would bear the consequences of their opposition. These angels would be burned – all except Michael, their leader. The same thing happened to the angels led by Gabriel, who was the only one spared from his group. The third group of angels was under Libbiel's leadership, and he was no fool. He saw what happened to the others and warned his band of angels to do as God commanded. They made it clear to God that He had their full support and that they would watch over the humans and share everything they learned about them. At this point, God renamed Libbiel to Raphael to reflect that he played the role of Rescuer, having saved his angels with his advice. God called him the "Angelic Prince of Healing," in charge of all heavenly and earthly medicines.

Archangel Raphael Imagery, Symbols, and Seals

Raphael is sometimes depicted with a fish. Sometimes, there's a young boy with him, holding the fish. The Archangel could also put on a pilgrim's outfit, and when dressed this way, he may have a gourd or walking staff in his right hand. The fish, pilgrim's outfit, and boy are drawn from the story of Raphael leading Tobias to Media and back home. Usually, the angel's hair is blonde, and sometimes it's a really dark shade of blonde. As a pilgrim, he'll sometimes wear a coat over a tunic that may have a flowing mantle. Raphael always has winged. When he shows up, his light is bright and infused with gold.

Archangel Raphael is often depicted with a young boy holding a fish.
Saint Raphael the Archangel. Colour lithograph. Raphael (Archangel). Work ID: gza6qtuq, Creative Commons Attribution (CC BY 4.0) <https://creativecommons.org/licenses/by/4.0/> https://www.lookandlearn.com/history-images/YW032933VEL/Saint-Raphael-the-Archangel

Raphael's color is emerald or moss green. Little wonder since this is the color of harmony and healing and the color of the heart chakra or energy center. Others consider bright green, purple, and gold his colors, too. Of the four classical elements, Raphael corresponds to Earth. The Caduceus is his symbol, which makes sense since he is the Patron of all healers. The sigil of Archangel Raphael has a cross in the middle, with a small circle on top and a slightly larger circle at the bottom. To the left and right of the cross are two vertical lines with small circles on top of each one, and their bottoms are connected by a horizontal line that runs through the bottom of the cross in the middle. To the left and right of this U shape, boxing off the cross, are two small crosses with equal vertical and horizontal lines. Another cross with equal lines rests above the middle traditional Christian cross.

At the bottom of the sigil is another cross with equal vertical and horizontal lines but with a small circle on top. To the left and right of this final cross are two Xs. All of these parts are contained in a circle. Around the circle, you have the words RAPHAEL on top, ADONAY to the right, OTHEOS at the bottom, and AGIOS to the left. Adonay means "Lord" or "Master," Otheos means "God," and Agios means "sacred." Each of these words has a small cross with equidistant lines in between them. Another circle binds these words on the outside.

Now you know all you need to know about who Archangel Raphael is. The question is, when is it okay to call upon him? And how would you even do that? You will learn about all this and more in the next chapter.

Chapter Two: When and How to Call Upon Archangel Raphael

Healing Your Body

No one does a better job than Archangel Raphael when it comes to physical healing. God has blessed him to help you heal in any way you need. Just a touch from Raphael can bring relief and restoration to whatever is out of alignment with your body. As a human, it is only natural that you experience some physical pain occasionally. Raphael, a very compassionate being, has been tasked with bringing you relief. His healing energy is reminiscent of a soothing breeze as it sweeps through your body and removes whatever plagues you.

Many have suffered chronic illnesses and have called upon Archangel Raphael, asking him to intercede on their behalf. Naturally, Raphael swoops in to answer their prayers. More than any physician, he understands what needs to be addressed in the mortal body to bring it back to a flawless state. The beautiful thing about this Archangel is that there is no judgment in his treatment. Not only is he excellent at healing the body of whatever it's going through, but he's also adept at bringing on a state of balance. By calling upon Archangel Raphael, you will experience a sense of wellness you have never known before. This being carries within him a celestial grace that flows into your body, harmonizes all its functions, fixes all that is fractured, and balances all disruptions in the systems within you.

When calling upon Raphael for healing, you must understand that you also have a part to play. For Raphael's healing work to take root, you must surrender to him completely. You must trust that his power can work with your body to create the desired results. It does no good for you to think negatively while calling him for help.

If you think of ill health and negativity, your body picks up on that and draws more bad energy. When you call on Raphael, and he attempts to use his healing energy on you, you will run into a few hiccups that you are responsible for. You must also make the right choices and do the right thing to be a conscious co-creator with Raphael to generate the desired health.

When you're in the presence of Raphael, his healing energy is unmistakable. Learn to tap into that and pay attention to the intuitive nudges you receive. He will use your intuition to communicate how you can improve your condition. You must realize this is a collaborative effort and act like it.

Healing Your Heart

Healing doesn't just occur on a physical level. There are times in life when you need your heart mended. You can reach out to Archangel Raphael to help you with this. The journey of emotional healing is a rhythmic one between light and darkness. It is about understanding that there is pain within your heart and accepting it while at the same time doing your best to stoke the flames of hope in your heart. Raphael can offer you the guidance and solace you need to restore your heart. Archangel Raphael can show you the way to set yourself free emotionally. He has no trouble with you displaying vulnerability, so don't assume that you must meet him in a somber, controlled manner. This Archangel offers the strength needed to battle your shadows and undo the twisted webs of emotions that keep you stuck and bound.

Healing Relationships

Raphael also has the power to heal and restore your relationships. Inevitably, everyone experiences misunderstandings. Sometimes, these misunderstandings can escalate to the point where a previously wonderful relationship is destroyed. However, there is no relationship or connection that Raphael cannot fix. So, call on him if you have a relationship that needs fixing.

Raphael has the power to heal any troubled relationship.
https://unsplash.com/photos/AsahNlC0VhQ

Healing Trauma

Trauma is an unfortunate aspect of being human. Sometimes, it may seem impossible to extricate yourself from the damage caused by traumatic events. However, being a divine being, Archangel Raphael can help you get through whatever trauma you may face. Also, trauma has been known to take away your sense of inner peace and make it impossible for you to feel safe. This impossibility thrives because you have not called upon divine support to help you. Raphael is an excellent inner guide that can keep you at peace amid the storm. If you learn nothing else from this section of the book, remember this: There isn't a thing on earth or anywhere else that Raphael cannot fully and completely heal.

Inspiring Creativity

Sometimes, you find your creative spirit trapped behind an inexplicable block. You do everything conventional knowledge says to shake yourself free of the mud. However, nothing works. Whenever you find yourself in this situation, call on Archangel Raphael. He, more than any other being, can lead you toward a world of infinite creative expression. He possesses the celestial melody that will sing your soul into full creative flow.

Archangel Raphael is known as the celestial muse. He knows how to help you turn your blank canvas into the most vibrant artwork. He knows how to guide your hand so that your empty page is transformed into literary genius. When you seek Raphael's assistance, you learn that creativity is not something you go after on your own. It is not a journey that you must go on alone. By opting to work with the divine, you tap into a realm of great ideas many people are unaware of. As a result, the works you create from this realm are literally out of this world.

So, call on Raphael to help you find your creative flow. Taking you by the hand through your intuition, he'll show you how to release yourself from the prison that is your comfort zone so that you can be at peace with the unknown that houses every creative idea you seek. Also, you can allow his energy to flow through you so you are not forcing things to happen. Instead, you let him flow through you to express divine creativity. In other words, you serve as a channel for divine inspiration. When you experience this flow, time ceases to exist. Not only that, but it also appears as though you could do your work forever. Often, those working with Raphael for inspiration and creativity report that by the time they are done creating their work, it feels like they have nothing to do with it. They were simply along for the ride.

Another thing to consider when it comes to creativity is the balance between taking risks and sticking to convention out of fear. When you find yourself amid this uncertainty, it becomes difficult to flow creatively. You'll notice that fear takes control of your heart and prevents you from exploring the world within you. When your creative work is full of self-doubt and hesitation, it's difficult not to see that. However, Raphael can unfurl his wings and swoop down to your rescue so that you can find the audacious spirit within you. You see, Raphael does not doubt what you can accomplish. He will help you remove the self-doubt and fear that make you hesitant to try new things with your work. He will encourage you to be bold about your writing, painting, or whatever else you do. Proficient at binding demons, Raphael will rope the ones that plague you on the inside and toss them into the abyss, allowing you to tap into the powerful emotions that drive your creativity. Now, do not assume this means you will never be afraid. Raphael will give you the ability to act despite that fear. Therefore, with time, you will realize that fear is nothing to fear when it comes to your creative work.

Helping Pets

It feels painful for both of you when you have an inexplicably ill pet. Naturally, these pets are family to you, so you want them to feel better. Raphael can help your pet too. You can turn to him to intervene. With his celestial light, he will heal your pet.

The only other thing as heart-wrenching as your being sick is losing them. In times like these, Raphael can act as a beacon that allows your pet to find its way home.

Overcoming Addictions

Addictions can leave you unable to see anything good about yourself. Raphael can offer you the strength to break free of the chains of addiction. As a celestial being, Raphael has a unique point of view on human complexities, particularly when it comes to struggles that appear outside your control. Better than any counselor on earth, Raphael feels the pain you go through and approaches the process of helping you heal with love and zero judgment. Does this imply you should not seek professional mental health therapy? Absolutely not. However, working with Archangel Raphael can help you get where you need to go faster.

Often, addiction can be rooted in trauma, emotional pain, or disconnection from your spiritual self. Raphael can heal the wounds that drive your destructive habits. You see, it is not enough to tell yourself that you will stop being addicted to something. You must address the hidden root causes, and Raphael can expose them to the light so that you can finally do something about them. This Archangel can give you the willpower to push past the temptation to revert to destructive behavior. This is important to know because there will be times when you feel tempted to give in. Raphael will assure you that this does not mean you are a terrible or weak person. He will encourage you through these difficult times to make the right choices.

Raphael offers inspiration and guidance through your intuition. He creates synchronistic events in your life that lead to people who will assist you through your predicament. He lights up the path toward recovery. You don't need to understand exactly how you will arrive at that destination. All you must do is trust Raphael is hard at work to bring you out of the prison of addiction.

On top of that, he can help you restore balance to your life by showing you better habits and practices that you can adopt to replace and totally eliminate your addictions. He can remove all the negative influences that encourage you to indulge in those addictions. When you need to cut off toxic relationships, this Archangel backs you up. He can help you with the resources to move out of negative environments that fuel your addictive behavior. On an energetic level, he can cut the cords that have bound you to places, people, and addictive substances that have ruled and ruined your life. Therefore, it would be best to seek Raphael when struggling with something addictive. The substance or behavior and how strongly attached you are to it do not matter. Raphael can set you on the right path regardless.

Assistance with Travel

Raphael is an excellent travel companion. He offers safety and protection in the air or on the road. You can have him safeguard your travels by ensuring you won't have any delays or accidents. Also, if there are multiple routes to your destination, but you're unsure of which one to take, you can reach out to him and ask him to pick the best one for you. Even in an unfamiliar place, he can guide you.

There are countless situations where people find themselves in travel emergencies, and, calling on Raphael, he came through for them. You should know that no matter how difficult a trip is, he will intervene and make the journey easier for you. All you have to do is ask him.

Summoning Archangel Raphael

Now that you know all the situations where Raphael can help you, how do you get his assistance? You need to summon him. There are several ways you can do that. Look at the following methods, and work with each one until you know what works best and feels right to you.

Prayer

Prayer is a holy bridge that connects you to the divine. When you pray, you craft a space of sacredness within your heart that acts as a sanctuary for your intentions to gain momentum and where they are projected into higher realms. With prayer, you can invite Raphael to your life and ask him to work his magic on you.

Various resources on the internet and other books will recommend specific prayers to use in summoning Raphael. However, there is really no specific template that you must follow. All you have to do is speak from your heart about your desire and believe your prayer has been heard.

Prayer is one of the most effective ways to summon Archangel Raphael.
https://unsplash.com/photos/ReEqHw2GyeI

Meditation and Visualization

Meditation is excellent for summoning Archangel Raphael when you need his help. Visualization involves bringing up specific scenes in your imagination. It will be a part of most of the other methods of summoning Raphael that you'll learn in this book. If you can imagine holding a golf ball in your hand or biting into a lemon, you have visualization skills.

Before you meditate, make you're somewhere free of distractions. Nothing and no one must disturb or interrupt you. You'll need to be in total silence for ten to fifteen minutes. Also, you must put on comfortable clothing.

1. Sit in a posture you can maintain during your meditation.
2. Close your eyes, and allow the world to fade so you tune in to your inner reality.
3. Inhale deeply, exhale slowly, and allow the day's burdens to fly away from you.
4. Notice your weight against the chair or floor, and feel your connection to the earth.
5. Continue breathing deeply until you notice your thoughts are still.

6. If your mind keeps wandering away from your breath, that's fine and nothing to feel frustrated about. Even if it happens a lot, notice that your attention has wandered, and then gently return your focus to your breath. In time, the stillness will come.
7. When your mind feels still, it's time to ask Raphael to come to you. You can state this intention aloud or simply sit with a feeling of expectancy as if you know now that he will grace you with his presence.
8. As you breathe and wait, imagine a brilliant emerald light with the radiance of a thousand sun-kissed leaves. See it flooding the room and space around you and flowing into your body.
9. Feel the energy of this light as it goes into every cell, awakening every fiber of your being. This is the Archangel's presence, love, light, and healing power. You are now connected to Raphael.

Using Mantras

Mantras are words, sounds, or phrases used to deepen a meditative state or summon celestial beings. While in meditation, you can use mantras to summon Raphael. First, focus on your breath, and when you notice you're still, begin repeating a simple mantra like, *"Raphael, please come to me now."* Your mantra can be whatever you want.

Using Chakras

Your chakras are energy portals that allow life force to flow into you on every level of existence. They also allow energy to flow out of you, affecting your life and even the lives of others around you. You can use these energy centers to summon Raphael.

1. Start by sitting or lying down somewhere comfortable and quiet.
2. Close your eyes, inhale, and exhale a few times as you bring your attention to the present moment and push distracting thoughts away.
3. Bring your attention to your heart chakra, the Anahata. See it as a pulsating, rotating portal of emerald, green energy.
4. In your mind or out loud, repeat Raphael's name. The intention behind this is to draw his presence. While doing this, notice how your heart chakra becomes more active as the light becomes more intense, brilliant, and warm, traveling through your being. This means you have established a connection to Raphael.

Using Reiki

Here's how to work with Reiki to get Archangel Raphael's assistance.

1. Go somewhere without any distractions or noises.
2. Cleanse the space. You can burn incense, light candles, ring a bell, or use any other method to clear out the energy of your workspace.
3. Ground yourself by sitting comfortably, closing your eyes, and focusing on taking deep breaths. As you breathe, imagine roots growing from where you're connected to the floor into the earth.
4. In your mind's eye, see a beam of light from the sky pouring into the top of your head, connecting you with divinity.
5. Set your intention to draw Archangel Raphael's presence to help you during your Reiki session. You can state this intention out loud as an invocation. Invite him to be present and empower your ritual.
6. Place your hands on your body (or that of the person you're trying to help), and in your mind's eye, see healing green light flowing through your hands. Trust that this light belongs to Raphael and that he is now here with you. You'll learn more about Reiki in a later chapter.

Free Writing and Art

Free writing is a way to allow the consciousness of Archangel Raphael to flow through you and get direct insight into whatever situation you're dealing with. You can also allow Raphael to flow through you using art. Here's how to do it:

1. First, find somewhere distraction-free. You'll need to sit at a comfortable desk for this one.
2. Intend to connect with Raphael. Be clear that you want to do this through free writing or art and seek guidance, help, health, or whatever else you need him to help you with.
3. Meditate for a few minutes or until you feel the stillness within you and your mind and body relax. Infuse your body and space with Raphael's light.
4. Open your eyes, hold your pen over your pad (or just sit with the tools of your preferred art medium, whatever that is), and breathe deeply.

5. Let the words or images flow through you. Don't try to think about whether they're actual words, what your handwriting looks like, or why you appear only to be doodling or something. If you're making art, imagine that your hands aren't yours. Instead, see them as Raphael's. Trust that his energy flows through you, and keep your awareness of your connection. It also helps to keep your focus on the paper so you don't get too analytical about your writing or creating.
6. You can ask a question and wait for your hand to begin writing. It is important to stay open throughout this process.
7. When you're done, thank Raphael. You can read and review what you got after the session and make any additional notes you like that come to mind. If you made art, you could sit with it and meditate on the goal of your practice.

Using Dreams and Astral Projection

Dreams are an excellent way to reach out to Archangel Raphael, making it easier for him to show up in all his glory. Astral projection involves leaving your physical body to explore the astral realms (and other realms) where you can gain knowledge, meet other beings, go places, and so on. Here's how you can have him work with you in your dreams.

1. Begin by setting your intention to connect with Raphael before bed. Be clear about what you'd like him to help you with.
2. Make sure that your room is conducive so that you can sleep well. It must be silent, completely dark (or at least with a nice, relaxing ambiance), and at a comfortable temperature. You can set the mood with some music if you like.
3. Before you drift off to sleep, wind down by meditating. This will clear your mind and keep you focused on your task.
4. As you meditate, envision Raphael's rich emerald green light around you and your room.
5. Say a prayer or make an affirmation to have him present as you go to sleep.
6. Have a pen and dream journal by your bed so you can write down what you remember after waking up.
7. While you drift off to sleep, repeat, *"Thank you, Raphael."*

8. When you wake up, don't move your body. If you do, return to being still as soon as possible, and don't open your eyes.
9. Think of the last thing you saw or what you felt, and this should kickstart the process of remembering what happened.
10. When you've got it all remembered, write keywords to represent each aspect of the dream first and then flesh out each one with details after.

What about astral projection? Here's how to go about it.

1. Set your intention to leave your body and meet Archangel Raphael.
2. Set your alarm for two to three hours before the usual time to get up, then go to bed.
3. When your alarm goes off, turn it off, get out of bed, and drink some water.
4. Take five to thirty minutes to read about astral projection and Archangel Raphael while intending you're going to meet with him in the astral plane.
5. Now, go back to bed, fixing the intention firmly in your mind that you'll leave your body.
6. When you sense you're awake, don't open your eyes or move your body. Instead, just sit up with your astral body and get out. The important thing is not to think too much. You may feel vibrations but don't stick around for those. Instead, leave your body, and get as far away from it as possible.
7. Intend to see Raphael. If he's not already there, you will find him eventually. From there, you can commune with him about whatever you need.
8. As you return to your body, scream one word that summarizes what he was saying (or a short phrase), as this will help you remember what he told you.
9. Don't hurry to get out of bed, open your eyes, or move when you wake up because your astral memories must be allowed to move from your astral mind to your physical one, and you must not interrupt that process. Otherwise, you will forget everything that happened.

10. When you can recall everything (thanks to the phrase or word you yelled out as you reentered your body), you can write it down in your dream journal.

Now that you know how to summon Archangel Raphael, you probably want to know how you can tell that this celestial being is present. The next chapter will teach you the signs that the Divine Healer is with you.

Chapter Three: Signs That Archangel Raphael Is Present

It may seem unlikely that you can interact with beings from other worlds. However, you should not dismiss the fact that you can have a true encounter with Archangel Raphael. But how could you possibly tell when you are in the presence of this wonderful celestial being? You must know the signs that he has arrived and has answered your prayer.

It is important to know that signs aren't only tangible things you can observe with your five senses. Signs of Archangel Raphael's presence can come in infinite ways. However, without exception, you know he is present because of an unmistakable gut feeling. Knowing these signs will comfort you when you experience them. You will have an unshakable faith that whatever you seek Raphael's help for will be a done deal.

Feathers

Many have seen feathers around them as a sign that the Archangel Raphael is present. He has a way of ensuring you spot these feathers at just the right place and time. In other words, a regular feather at any other place or time may not catch your eye or strike your heart. Still, when it is a clear sign from Raphael, you'll know it because, instantly, you will freeze and understand what you're looking at.

Spotting a feather at the right place and time indicates that Raphael is with you.
https://www.pexels.com/photo/grayscale-photo-of-feather-1320724/

Someone else seeing that same feather won't even look twice. However, you know better. You know that that feather is celestial. It is important not to take the sign lightly because it symbolizes that you have got Archangel Raphael's attention and that whatever you have brought to him to be handled is being worked on. You may think of these feathers as reminders that you are not alone. You have the hosts of Raphael right by your side, ready to assist you.

A Feathery Message to Samantha

Here's Samantha's encounter with Raphael:

> *"I had just moved out of a lovely apartment I once shared with my partner, only to downgrade to somewhere in a terrible neighborhood. I was also at a loss about what to do concerning my lower back, which had become a serious problem. I had to sit for extended periods as a writer to create content. This meant I could not write fast enough to make enough money to move somewhere better, and my back's protests had grown from low grumbles to deafening roars of pain.*

One day, I watched a YouTube video about reaching out to Archangel Raphael for healing. I thought it couldn't possibly hurt as I was really suffering. So, I said a simple prayer. And then, I forgot all about it and did my best to make the most of my new life. The next day, I walked around my new neighborhood, cautiously watching everyone around me. I realized I was a little too on edge and longed for the days when I could walk care-free.

As I almost broke down in tears, barely keeping it together, I noticed a white feather floating down from above. Right then and there, I stopped in my tracks. As it floated down, I reached out with my palm, and it settled down on it. The moment the feather touched my hand, I felt intense relief. It was as though I had been walking around with a boulder around my shoulders, and someone had suddenly lifted that load off me. I couldn't explain it, but I knew everything would be okay.

For the first time in months, I went to bed comfortably with no back pain. I woke up the next day feeling amazing. Just a couple of weeks later, I got a phone call from a production company that would radically change my life. They bought a TV show that I had been pitching unsuccessfully for the past two years. The company offered me an amount of money that I had never before imagined having. Working with an agent, I decided to ask for more. I did just that, and a week after that, I had more than enough money to move out of that dangerous apartment and into somewhere that was more my speed. I kept that feather as a reminder that angels are real, and if you ask them, they're ready to help you with whatever you need."

Angel Numbers

Have you ever looked at the clock, and a sequence of numbers caught your attention? These numbers show up not just on the clock, but on license plates, in conversations, on price tags, coded serial numbers, and so on. In fact, you may have noticed that you have a penchant for waking up at a particular time every day without an alarm clock.

If you have noticed these numbers popping up often, you may have combed the internet to determine what they mean. You may have found some information claiming these numbers should not be taken seriously. Those who hold this position claim that the numbers you notice are only a result of your reticular activating system, a brain process responsible for helping you find patterns in things. They'll tell you that it's the reason why when you buy a red car, for instance, you suddenly start noticing red cars everywhere.

But you get the sense that there's a lot more to these numbers than what you're being told. The truth is you are right. These numbers aren't ordinary. They are known as angel numbers. They could be repetitive ones like 111, 222, 333, or any other number appearing in threes or fours (or even larger groups). The numbers could be 1010, 411, 414, 717, 8080, etc. It doesn't matter how they show up. What matters is that when they do, you get the sense that the world stops. Whatever thought process you had going on then suddenly becomes irrelevant. You are heavily rooted in the here and now and so grounded that it almost feels as if life is literally a dream or a simulation. You feel this way because the angel Raphael is making his presence known. He is showing you that there are forces and powers beyond physical reality's seeming rigidity and changelessness.

When these numbers show up, you are meant to take advantage of that feeling of unrealness by planting the seed of whatever you desire in your mind. How do you do this? By accepting that no matter how seemingly impossible your desires are, anything under the sun can be accomplished through divine means. And, you have the divine means because you have the support of Raphael and his host of angels. For some people, that's not enough. If this is you, the following section briefly explains the meaning of every number from 0 through 9. Suppose you see number sequences that are a combination of various numbers. In that case, all you have to do is take the meanings of each individual number, and combine them, then apply them to your life.

Numbers and Their Meanings

- **Zero** is the number of infinite potentials. It stands for the divine connections you have. Seeing this number is as if you're being asked to remain in the present. Call your attention and energy from the past and the future and bring them to the here and now. In this moment and space, Raphael advises you to let go of old attachments and allow yourself to move with the flow of divinity, trusting that the unknown is wonderful and will lead you to your highest ideals.

- **One** is the number of divine inspirations. It's about new beginnings and the power of manifestation. When you run into a number sequence with ones in it, Raphael tells you that you must embrace the strength within and accept your potential to create greatness.
- **Two** is the number of duality. It expresses the concept of partnerships and balance. When you see number two in a number sequence, Raphael asks you to do what you can to encourage harmonious relationships. He also wants you to find harmony within yourself. Number two tells you that you must feed the healthy connections that you have in life and balance your emotions.
- **Three** is the number of creative energy. It is the presence of guidance from above. Whenever a number sequence has a 3, you are asked to acknowledge divinity's presence in your life. Also, you are called to be bold about expressing yourself creatively and living from a place of authenticity. Number three asks you to embrace your unique talents and let go of the doubt that keeps you from fully expressing them so that you can reach new heights.
- **Four** is the number of stability. It represents the idea of being supported. When this number appears in an angel number sequence, Raphael is encouraging you out of uncertainty. He would like you to be more trusting of the universe and its natural rhythms. Four calls you to recognize that you are part of nature, which means you could never be in the wrong place at the wrong time. You must trust that the flow of nature will bring you exactly where you need to go.
- **Five** is the number of freedom change and transformation. When five appears in an angel number sequence, you are asked to be open to future changes. It tells you that you must let go of the old to accept the new miracles you have prayed for and desired for the longest time. Five asks you to be at peace regardless of how chaotic this change may be because, inevitably, it will lead you to where you want to be.
- **Six** is a number that many assume is negative. That is mainly because of the Christian interpretation of the number 666, which is said to be the mark of the evil beast. However, this is

not the case when it comes to angel numbers. The number six in an angel number sequence is basically a message asking you to dig below the surface of things so that you can discover the truth of your situation. It calls for destroying and tearing down all illusions that keep you bound to your present, undesirable reality. Six asks you to find the balance point in the confusion and chaos and to reconnect with the divinity that you carry. It reminds you that the light will emerge no matter how dark things may seem.

- **Seven** is a divine number. It represents inner wisdom, intuition, and awakening to your spiritual self. When you see the number 7 in an angelic number sequence, you're called to pay attention to what your soul tells you. Your life is aligned with a divine plan, and you must trust that there is wisdom within you greater than what you are aware of. Seven asks you to trust your intuition and to allow Raphael to show you the way to go.
- **Eight** is the number of success, abundance, and infinite possibilities. Seeing eight in a number sequence means you are being or about to be immensely blessed. It's a sign that everything around you is lining up to favor you in the best way possible. Expect many open doors when this number begins to appear in your life. Expect the unexpected. You know the saying, "It's too good to be true?" Well, you can expect that the good things to come your way will be better than you could have imagined, and they will be true. Remember, you must share the abundance in your life because giving means receiving even more.
- **Nine** is a powerful number representing spiritual alignment, completing things, and finding closure. When nine is in an angel number sequence, Raphael is leading you through the last stages of a situation or the final chapters of a certain book in your life. Nine is the number of endings. Endings are not necessarily bad because they can and do lead to new beginnings. So, when you notice this number, let go of whatever you're dealing with and trust that all things will be reborn. You'll experience a new life cycle, leading to the evolution of your higher self, affecting you positively in every way.

Siobhan's Saving Numbers

Here's Siobhan's story:

"777 has always shown up for as long as I can remember. It's been a guide of sorts. However, when I learned about Archangels, I developed a strong interest in Raphael. The more I learned about this Archangel, the more I saw 777. It reached the point where I could trust that unless I saw 777, I would not act on any major decision I had to make.

One day, I had to make a trip. I had a dream the previous night about my plane crashing. So, when I woke up the next day, I felt some trepidation, but I honestly felt like I had no choice but to go since it was a work trip. I arrived at the airport and saw a truck with the number 777 on its license plate. I felt good seeing the number until I saw what was written on the side of the truck. The words "back home" were boldly staring back at me. Immediately, I asked the driver to take me back.

Later that night, I was watching the news. It turned out that the flight I was supposed to be on wound up crashing just before it could land. More than ever, I am certain that that warning was from Angel Raphael himself. That night, I took a moment to thank Raphael for his protection."

Emerald Green Everywhere

Emerald green contains Raphael's essence. Many people who encountered this Archangel claim that they saw emerald green. Sometimes, it could be a light that isn't detectable by everyone other than the person it's meant for. Other times, something emerald green is in the person's surroundings.

You may have a dream where that color is predominant in the form of light, crystals, or nature. Usually, when you see it, it has a very profound effect on your consciousness. In other words, it affects you mentally and physically. So, it would be best to begin paying attention to emerald green. Not because you're trying to force it to appear, but just to acknowledge that each time you notice it, odds are Raphael is nearby.

Danielle Touched By an Angel

Marshall had been going through a lot since his wife was involved in a car accident. She lay in the hospital for 3 weeks, unconscious, despite the doctor's best efforts. Marshall did all he could to learn ways to help someone regain consciousness. However, he was quickly losing hope.

One day, Marshall stumbled across an article about how someone claimed to have connected with the Archangel Raphael. This person's story inspired him. He decided that he was going to reach out to the Archangel. Marshall was not a praying man. He did not believe in any reality outside of the physical, but he had tried everything at this point. Marshall was more than willing to try praying to this angel. How he saw it, no one was around to judge him for suddenly becoming a believer.

So, he knelt and prayed to Archangel Raphael on behalf of his wife. When he was done, he sat back down, feeling foolish. A few moments later, a nurse he had not seen before entered the room. She smiled at Marshall as she tended to his wife, Danielle. The nurse fluffed her pillow and arranged her body properly in bed. And then she did something Marshall thought was a bit weird. Still smiling at Marshall, the nurse touched Danielle's forehead briefly. And then she placed her hands on Danielle's chest for a few seconds. She turned to Marshall, smiled, and said, "You've been heard."

Then, just as Marshall was about to ask her who she was, the nurse walked out of the room. He noticed an odd flash of green light against the wall just as the nurse headed out the door. This left Marshall baffled. He turned to face his wife, and Danielle opened her eyes for the first time in 21 days.

Disappearing Symptoms

Disappearing symptoms don't always indicate Archangel Raphael's presence. There could be other factors, such as your body naturally healing itself. However, those who have called on Archangel Raphael to help them with their afflictions usually report that they've noticed a reduction in the intensity of their symptoms. Do not be alarmed if you notice this happening when you seek help. It is important to state here that you should always seek out the help of a medical professional in addition to working with Archangel Raphael to confirm that your condition is indeed getting better.

Now that you know all the signs that Archangel Raphael is present and that he's listening, it's time to look at how you can enlist his help to overcome negative thoughts and emotions. Read the next chapter to learn how Raphael can help you take charge of your emotional and mental well-being.

Chapter Four: Healing Negative Thoughts and Emotions

Praying to Archangel Raphael or connecting with him in any other way does not imply you do not need to see a doctor. Raphael can help you with the healing process. Still, it doesn't hurt to do your part and be responsible for your health by going to the hospital when something is wrong with you or a loved one.

Archangel Raphael is known as the Angelic Prince of Healing. He isn't limited to helping with physical health issues but also your emotions, thoughts, and spirit. The question is, why would you need healing on any other level besides the physical one? Do the wounds that can't be seen with your eyes matter? In fact, do they even exist? Yes, they do, and their effects are damaging.

The Effects of Automatic Negative Thoughts

Automatic negative thoughts, also called ANTs, are insidious ideas that enter the mind and take over if left unchecked, leading you to criticize yourself harshly, live a life full of fear, and constantly doubt your abilities. These thoughts make you feel like you're not good enough and that even through blood, sweat, and tears, you just won't succeed. The voice in your head tells you that you don't deserve to be happy, you shouldn't be loved, and that all good things must eventually come to an end - assuming you were ever lucky enough to experience good, to begin with. These thoughts fuel emotions such as sadness, resentment, scorn, anger, pain, and guilt, making it tough for you to live a life full of passion and purpose.

Some studies suggest that intrusive negative thoughts can also affect your health. According to an article titled The Automaticity of Positive and Negative Thinking: A Scoping Review of Mental Habits by Colvin et al., in Cognitive Therapy and Research, thinking negative thoughts, criticizing yourself and others, and constantly worrying about things can lead to terrible mental health. There's also another study in the BMC Public Health by Grobosch et al., 2021, titled Thoughts about health and patient-reported outcomes among people with diabetes mellitus: results from the DiaDec-study, where the researchers discovered that those with diabetes mellitus who had a pattern of negative thinking would wind up having other health issues to contend with.

When you have a constant barrage of negative thoughts and emotions in your head, your body suffers stress too. Your bloodstream gets flooded with cortisol, which spikes your heart rate and blood pressure to concerning levels and causes your muscles to grow tense. These are natural responses to have when dealing with a threat, but when your body cannot turn off these responses, this can cause issues with your cardiovascular health and leave you with a flawed immune system. As for your mental abilities, you'll find it tough to be creative or to find the drive to go after your desires. You'll have a distorted idea of what's real versus what isn't, making it impossible to take practical actions that could change your life. Also, negative thoughts and emotions are the primary drivers of bad habits that keep you captive and make it hard to choose the right thing to elevate your life and uplift your soul. The following are some of the thoughts and emotions Archangel Raphael can you with.

Anxiety

Living with anxiety is like constantly being caught in a storm that refuses to let up. It always feels dark, foreboding, and heavy. People who struggle with anxiety have a difficult time just breathing. Often, situations that shouldn't be a big deal overwhelm individuals who struggle with anxiety. It doesn't matter if your anxiety is about where the bills will come from or a trip you must take. It always feels crippling and has a firm grasp on your heart, putting you in a place of no escape. Anxiety makes it difficult to feel free. It is a relentless emotion when you give in to it.

Archangel Raphael can help you navigate the storms of anxiety. Thanks to his healing power, and soothing presence, you can call on him to shield you from the things that cause you discomfort. Better than that, he can help you find the strength to persevere through whatever you're going through. Say you find yourself on an airplane, and you've always been nervous about flying. You can call on Archangel Raphael to help you manage your anxious emotions. You may notice that the anxiety is still there, but you feel more at peace with it and can just observe it as though it were a guest in your mind. By helping you see anxiety this way, Raphael shows you that you don't have to identify with the emotion just because you feel it. He helps you understand that emotions are transient and they are not your identity.

Ritual for Anxiety

Whenever you feel anxious, you can do this ritual anywhere:

1. Find a quiet place where you won't be distracted or disturbed.
2. Take a moment to ground yourself. Close your eyes, take a few deep breaths, and focus on the present moment.
3. Set your intention to call upon Archangel Raphael. Your intention should be clear. In this case, you want to seek his help to overcome crippling anxiety.
4. In your mind's eye, imagine a brilliant emerald light that surrounds you. Feel this light as it energizes your body from head to toe. Allow the healing light of Archangel Raphael to wash through you.
5. As you breathe in, allow this light to flow into your lungs and spread to every part of your body.
6. As you exhale, imagine your anxiety is a cloud of black energy that emerges through your slightly parted lips with each exhale.
7. As you continue breathing, feel this anxiety in your belly or your chest continuing to fade away with each exhale.
8. At this point, you should feel more at ease and grounded. You should feel an unmistakable sense of calm.
9. Use affirmations to boost the calm and peace you feel within if you want to. You can use a simple affirmation like, *"I am calm now. I am at ease now. "*

10. Take a moment to thank Raphael for helping you and showing up as he always does.
11. Bring your attention back to your breath and allow it to ground you briefly before you open your eyes. Understand that when you leave that space, you will carry Raphael's green, calming light with you.

Once more, it is important to remember that you can use this ritual anytime, anyplace.

Work Stress

You live in a world where it is natural to be stressed out about work. So heavy is the burden of work on your soul that it taints everything you do. You start as a vibrant child, eager to explore life, learn new things, and offer your gifts to the world. At some point, however, life finds a way to weigh you down. The system currently in sway in this world is not conducive to play. It finds a way to take the most enjoyable things about life and make them feel like drudgery. The inevitable result is that you wind up feeling extremely stressed. Even when you return from work, those precious few hours before you have to do it again the next day are tainted by the stress from the office or your business. Unfortunately, most people don't know how to handle this stress effectively, so they take it out on their loved ones, picking up bad habits to feel good.

You can call on Raphael to help you handle stress. He does an excellent job of reminding you of the strength that you carry within you. Also, he can set things up so that you're no longer as stressed as you used to be before you called on him for assistance. Another thing he can do for you is to help you find your love and passion for what you do once more. Usually, when people find a job that aligns with their ideals, it feels like they're not even working. If you are in a situation that needs to change, Raphael can help you deal with this so you can be less stressed about your purpose in life. If you are exactly where you need to be, he can help you change your perspective so that you can begin to appreciate your work.

Ritual for Work Stress

You should perform this ritual either at the start of your day or at the end.

1. Begin by finding somewhere quiet. You will need at least 10 to 15 minutes by yourself.
2. Close your eyes, part your lips slightly, and take a deep inhale through your nose. Exhale gently through your parted lips. As you breathe, allow your body and mind to relax and be rooted in the moment.
3. Now, it's time to invoke the presence of Archangel Raphael. You can do this by saying, "Archangel Raphael, please come to me now with your healing and love. Guide me so I can let go of stress and experience more bliss and peace in life."
4. In your mind, imagine Raphael's brilliant emerald light. See this light as it shimmers around the room, gradually approaching you. Feel it as it wraps itself all around you. You should feel more relaxed and soothed. This light is full of tranquility and peace.
5. As you exhale through your slightly parted lips, allow all the tension and stress you feel in your body and mind to melt away. If you feel like you are bombarded with negative thoughts about work, do not try to fight them. Instead, notice them as you would birds flying outside the window. Understand that the birds will only be there briefly, and allow your negative thoughts to flow away.
6. You can now use affirmations at this point to reaffirm your peace and tranquility. You can simply say, *"I now let go of all the stress I once felt. I now open myself to Raphael's calmness and peace."*
7. Thank the Archangel for showing up and helping you work through the stress.
8. With one last inhale and exhale, gently open your eyes and feel your awareness return to the room. You can now carry a sense of calmness and tranquility into your day.

Regardless of how packed your schedule is for the day or where you are, you can perform this ritual at any point to help you handle stress better than you ever thought possible.

Addiction

Addiction is so powerful that it is difficult even to realize you are an addict. Usually, addicts feel like they are locked away in a cell, and the keys have been tossed into a deep abyss, never to be found again.

Addiction causes you to self-sabotage. You may be addicted to patterns of behavior or substances that bring momentary relief but ultimately wreak havoc on your physical and mental health.

Addiction affects you in every way possible. It has you convinced that there's no option but to give in. It continues to thrive because of the fears you have. Everyone has insecurities, which are the perfect way for addiction to get a hold of you. You may have experienced something traumatic and painful in your past that has led you to your current state of mind. You find yourself helplessly dependent on certain behaviors or substances that drain your life force.

Thankfully, Archangel Raphael can lend his assistance in your recovery efforts. Once more, it is important to state that you must not attempt to deal with your addictions without the help of professionals. Do not assume that just because you've called upon a celestial being, you do not need anyone else's help. Instead, you can consider these professionals as Raphael's helpers and facilitators. He can help set you free.

The great thing about working with an Archangel, especially the Archangel of healing, is that he will illuminate the true sources of your addictive behavior. You see, it is not enough to simply decide to stop doing something. It is difficult to uncover where the drive to engage in these harmful practices comes from, let alone figure out how to address the core issue. But, working with Archangel Raphael, you will experience true, lasting healing. He will not just help you stop the addictive behavior but to heal the emotional wounds and trauma that led to it in the first place. As you recover, Raphael will give you all the strength and assistance you need to go through the treacherous journey of getting back to wholeness.

Ritual for Releasing Addictions

Whether the addictive behavior you are struggling with is binge eating, watching pornography, smoking, or something else, you can use this ritual to call upon Archangel Raphael to help you deal with it.

1. Find somewhere nice and quiet.
2. Light a white candle.
3. Sit or lie down in a comfortable position, and then close your eyes. Part your lips slightly.

4. Inhale through your nose and exhale through your lips. Continue until you feel fully present and focused.
5. Now, imagine the healing emerald light of Raphael flowing down to you from the sky and enveloping you from head to toe.
6. With the light surrounding you, boldly state your intention with sincerity in your heart. You must also completely trust Raphael to help you work on your addiction.
7. In your mind's eye, imagine the addiction you struggle with as a dark, heavy ball of energy that sits right in the middle of your chest. As you inhale, breathe in Raphael's light.
8. As you exhale, breathe out the addiction. Continue this process until you feel the ball getting lighter and lighter in color. The goal is to reach a point where the darkness is gone, and you are full of green, healing light.
9. Now, imagine yourself months or years from the present moment. Imagine that you have not indulged in addictive behavior for years. Feel the gratitude overwhelm you as it occurs to you that you have finally overcome what you once thought you could never beat.
10. Now, affirm the following: *"Archangel Raphael, I thank you. You have set me free, and forever I stay free."*
11. Thank Raphael for helping you to see what's possible and freeing you from the addiction.
12. Take one more inhale through your nose, exhale through your lips, and then gently open your eyes and return to the present.

Phobias

Everyone has a phobia that is difficult to explain, rationalize, or overcome. These fears are uncontrollable and beyond explanation. When faced with a phobia, you feel as if you have been caught in the stickiest web of terror. Raphael can teach you that there is nothing to fear except fear itself.

What exactly are phobias? They come from deep-seated experiences and memories that are the sources of intense traumas. Lacking the ability to deal with the traumatic experience when it happens, your mind pushes those memories into the subconscious, where you don't have to deal with them until you are reminded of that particular phobia. There are theories that some of the phobias that you deal with are not necessarily from your present incarnation but from a previous life. Regardless of the source, denying their powerful, sinister influence is impossible. They make it impossible for you to be truly free and, in debilitating cases, can stop you from accomplishing what you want in life. Phobias can steal your joy and make your days as dark as night.

You do not have to worry about this if you call upon Archangel Raphael to help you process the phobia. He is an excellent choice to help you overcome whatever terrifies you. He shines a light to illuminate that the shadows are not substantial and should not be feared. His loving, green light banishes all the monsters you imagine are on your path. Let's look at a ritual you can use to help you deal with phobias, with Archangel Raphael fighting your battles by your side.

Ritual for Phobias

1. Find somewhere free from distractions. You don't want to be disturbed during this ritual.
2. Light a white candle or a green one to represent the energy of Raphael and healing.
3. Close your eyes, slightly part your lips, inhale through your nose, and exhale through your mouth. Focus on bringing your awareness to the present moment.
4. In your mind's eye, imagine that the candle flame is green. See its light glowing brighter as you breathe. Imagine the green light engulfing you. It feels amazing, warm, soothing, and healing.
5. Now, call Raphael by saying or thinking, *"Raphael, Sweet Raphael, the Greatest Healer of All, I call upon you. I seek your love, protection, and help so that I may master my fear (mention the phobia you want him to help you get over). Please assist me. Set me free from this phobia. Show me how to be brave, strong, and courageous even when it stares me in the face."*
6. Imagine Raphael standing before you, glowing with a beautiful green light. Look into his penetrating yet loving eyes, and allow the power to wash over you.
7. Now, affirm as many times as you'd like, *"I now release every fear and accept love and healing into my life."*

8. Imagine you're faced with whatever you're afraid of and handling the situation with grace, confidence, and boldness with Raphael by your side.
9. Thank the Archangel for supporting and helping you handle your phobia. Trust that he will address it in the best way possible.
10. Take a few more deep breaths to return to the present, open your eyes and put out the candles, or let them burn as you feel gratitude for having handled your phobias.

Sadness, Grief, and Bereavement

Sadness happens to everyone. Sometimes, things won't go as planned. The dreams and goals you'd hoped to have accomplished by a certain time haven't come true yet. You lose something that means a lot to you, or you look around at the state of the world and find the events are appalling and unbelievable, weighing down on your spirit. Either way, this darkness touches one and all, and that's because, as a human being, you're vulnerable. You must remember that there's nothing permanent about sadness. It's like looking at the sky. No matter how hard you try to keep a cloud there, it will get swept away with time.

There is an upside to sadness, as tough as it may be to realize it when you're in its grasp. Sadness is there to teach you that there's something wrong. It shows you that you're carrying pain and that instead of acting like everything is fine, you must take the time to put down the pain and look at it. You must process what hurts you before you rise above it or stop it from defining you. Archangel Raphael can help you with the process of experiencing your sadness and gaining the strength and resilience to overcome the pain.

Grief and bereavement are more intense than sadness. For instance, you may lose someone close to your heart or a key job or relationship. Grief involves other emotions like despair, anger, guilt, and sadness. It's natural and unavoidable when dealing with loss, but sometimes, it can be hard to get out of the feeling of grief. If this is where you're at, know you can have Raphael's assistance. As for bereavement, it is the period after you've lost someone. You're in mourning. It will take as long as it takes, but when it's gotten to the point where you can no longer function even with therapy, divine intervention may just be what you need.

Meditation for Sadness, Grief, and Bereavement

The following is a simple ritual you can do to get Raphael to help you feel better when you're sad or when you need to let go of grief and bereavement.

1. Go somewhere quiet and free of distractions.
2. Light a green or white candle, and place it on a safe surface in front of you.
3. Get a pen and notepad.
4. Sit comfortably and close your eyes. Take some deep, grounding breaths.
5. As you get stiller in your mind, imagine brown roots growing from the bottom of your feet, going into the ground, and anchoring you to the earth's energy. Allow these roots to make you feel more stable and secure.
6. Invoke Archangel Raphael. Just make a simple statement inviting him to your space and letting him know you seek his comfort and assistance through this difficult time.
7. Open your eyes and turn to your journal. Start writing everything about the situation you're dealing with. The intention behind this exercise is to help you release your emotions. Do not be afraid to get it all. No one will read this besides you.
8. When you're done writing, read everything. You may feel the urge to cry if you weren't already doing so during the writing process. Know that tears are fine. You should read what you've written out loud, and as you do, be aware of how much it hurts and how heavy it feels.
9. It's time for you to release the pain. Hold the paper over the candle's flame with a pair of tongs, letting it catch fire. As the paper begins to burn, imagine in your mind's eye that it is everything that has held you down. Then, set it somewhere safe and let it continue burning.
10. Imagine that the smoke is being transformed into an emerald green light. As it rises and dissipates, allow yourself to feel the relief of having poured out your heart and transmuted your

sadness and pain into healing.
11. When the paper is done burning, go ahead and put out the candles.
12. Close your eyes. Imagine you're looking at this beautiful emerald light that is Raphael's signature. Imagine it surrounds you and begins to pour into your heart energy center. As this green light fills your heart, it dissolves and removes all the pain you feel.
13. Picture your heart glowing with green, emerald green light. That means your heart, body, and mind are healed too.
14. Thank Archangel Raphael for infusing your body, mind, and soul with his loving energy that heals and transforms you. You can thank him in your heart or out loud. The wonderful thing about doing this out loud is that you will feel the vibrations of healing and gratitude overwhelm your body.
15. Sit in the stillness as you bask in the emerald green glow from your heart and Raphael. When you are ready, open your eyes, and carry this energy with you throughout the day. You can repeat this ritual whenever you want, as often as you want.

Archangel Raphael can also help you handle troubled relationships. He will be more than happy to help. Dive deeper into this topic in the following chapter.

Chapter Five: Healing Relationships and Marriages

Archangel Raphael is known to be a matchmaker who helps people deepen their connections on a spiritual level. He's not just the master of healing but also of love, which makes sense as love is the energy that powers healing. That is why working with your heart chakra is always a good idea when doing any meditation, spell, or ritual involving healing and Raphael.

Archangel Raphael is known to be summoned to help heal relationships.
https://www.pexels.com/photo/man-and-woman-near-grass-field-1415131/

Facilitating Marital Unions

In the book of Tobit, Archangel Raphael helped Tobias and Sara with the demon so they could go on to enjoy a long-lasting and happy married life with each other. Now, your relationship may not be suffering because of actual evil entities. Still, the fact remains that when there are troubles between you and your partner, there is some darkness there. You could use the light of Raphael to illuminate the love that still lies between you so that you can recall why you both work so well in the first place. But more than that, if you've been single for quite a while and want someone to call your own, you can reach out to Raphael for assistance. He can set up a situation where you encounter someone meant for you. He isn't a matchmaker for nothing! You can ask for his assistance in finding the right one for you. Here is a simple meditation you can use to get Raphael to help you get the love of your life:

1. Find somewhere comfortable and quiet. Close your eyes, and take some grounding breaths.
2. In your mind's eye, imagine Raphael's green light surrounding you.
3. Now, imagine this green light transforming your space into a lush garden. In your mind, see Archangel Raphael approaching you with his wings stretched out wide.
4. Picture him reaching out to you with both hands, placing one on your chest where your heart is and the other on your head.
5. Imagine that from both his hands, healing, loving green energy flows into you through you.
6. Picture him taking his hands off you and your heart chakra blazing with emerald green light.
7. Imagine that this green light forms a straight line that travels out before you. Notice that in the distance in this large, magnificent garden is another person whose features you can barely make out. Notice that the straight green line of light from your heart flows towards this other person's heart on the other end of the garden.
8. Feel the sensation of being loved and loving someone. This other person on the other side of the garden is your destined partner.
9. Offer your thanks to Raphael.

10. When you are ready, take a few more grounding breaths as you gradually return your awareness to your physical reality and then open your eyes. Whenever you feel alone or wish someone was by your side, simply remember this exercise and let it reassure you that you have already connected to this person. They will be revealed to you at the right time.

Note: You can also use this exercise to strengthen your love for your partner if you're already married or in a relationship. In this case, visualize being in each other's arms and letting the green, loving light flow directly from one heart to the other.

Staying Faithful

Raphael can assist you when you're tempted to stray from your partner. Suppose you ever find yourself in a situation where your desire for someone else is overwhelming, or a third party has made it their mission in life to "get" you. In that case, you can ask Raphael to help you. This Archangel is aware that you are only human. He knows that complexities can arise and cause trouble even when the love is strong between you and your partner. One of the ways that he can help you with this is by getting you to reflect on your thoughts and emotions. He can also help you discover the external influences that make it hard for you to stay committed to your partner. He'll make it easier for you to communicate honestly with your significant other about your struggles. Communication is always key.

You can perform the following ritual to ensure you and your partner remain faithful to each other. For this exercise, you will need an emerald crystal. If you do not have one, use a quartz crystal instead.

1. First, find somewhere quiet where you will not be bothered for the next 10 to 15 minutes.
2. Prepare the space for your ritual using soft lighting and calm music. If you wish, you can incorporate crystals and candles.
3. Sit comfortably, and close your eyes. Take a few deep breaths to ground yourself in the moment.
4. Hold the emerald in your hands. As you breathe, imagine that you are establishing an energetic connection between yourself and the crystal. You can do this by seeing a brilliant emerald light coming out of the crystal flowing all around you and enveloping your body. Feel the energy of the crystal flow into and through

you.
5. Call upon Archangel Raphael. State your intention clearly and boldly by asking him to guide you through your ritual and offer you the energy and state of mind required to remain faithful to your partner. Also, state everything you desire regarding your relationship. All that matters is that you speak from your heart.
6. Imagine that Raphael's energy infuses your partner's heart and yours. Picture this energy forming a bond wrapping itself around you and your partner, bringing you closer together so that you become one. This energy will create loyalty, trust, and love between you.
7. Thank Raphael for his guidance and assistance.
8. Take a few more grounding breaths. Open your eyes when you feel ready. You'll find it helpful to carry the crystal wherever you go.

Navigating Conflict

When you're in a relationship, you'll inevitably butt heads with your partner occasionally. Unfortunately, not everyone has the right skills to navigate conflict successfully, and what should otherwise have been a small issue becomes something blown out of proportion that destroys a formerly beautiful union. When conflicts arise, Raphael can help quarreling partners deal with the situation in a way that allows each person to feel understood. His efforts encourage the love between both parties to grow stronger than ever. He makes it possible for troubling topics to be discussed in a way that allows compassion to flourish.

Often, conflicts can devolve to a point where each person only feels anger and resentment. With Raphael's help, he can give you the patience to hear your partner out and see things through their eyes, allowing more empathy and connection between you two. More than making it easy to talk to your partner, the matchmaking Archangel can also help you find ways in which your seemingly different perspectives intertwine and devise the best fixes that honor what each of you needs from the relationship. In other words, if you want things to always end on a win-win note, you should ask Raphael to intervene before you do anything else. Here is an excellent ritual that you can use to deal with conflict.
1. As always, the first thing you must do is create a sacred space that is quiet and free from distractions and disturbances. Remember,

you can set the mood by using soft lighting and ensuring the room is at the right temperature. Some soothing meditation music can also help.

2. Light a green candle. This candle is the representation of the harmony and healing that you seek between yourself and your partner. If you like, you can perform this ritual with your partner, but if they're not willing, you can still perform this on your own, trusting that you will get the results you seek.

3. Invoke Archangel Raphael. You may need to take a few deep, calming breaths while focusing on his emerald green light coming down from the sky and enveloping you.

4. When you feel his presence, you are ready to express your feelings about your partner. First, take each other's hands and hold them gently and lovingly. Express everything, including your frustrations, anger, and all the positive things you love about them. You need to get it all out there. If you are doing this exercise with your partner, they should also express how they feel. In this case, both of you must be respectful during the other's turn to talk. There is a way to communicate grievances without making the other person feel attacked. Be mindful of the words you choose, but speak your truth.

5. If tension is rising, you both must pause and take a few grounding breaths to bring you back to the intention of this ritual, which is to find unity and love once more. When tensions are hard to ignore, you can ask Raphael to intervene by bringing peaceful, calming energy. You can also imagine that the emerald light surrounding you grows in intensity, encouraging you both to be more compassionate and understanding toward each other.

6. When you are done sharing, imagine the emerald light emanating from your hands and flowing to your hearts. Then, picture the green light from each person's heart emanating and beaming towards the other, touching their heart. You are now in a loving, energetic cocoon. This is the melting and coming together point of your spirits, where they become one.

7. Take a few moments to appreciate what you love about each other. You can think about this in your mind, but it would be more beneficial to say the words aloud so your partner can hear and appreciate you too.

8. If you are performing this ritual alone, you can bring your partner's image to mind while you do it. You can hold their hands in your mind.
9. When you are ready, thank Raphael for assisting you.
10. Take a few calming, grounded breaths, and open your eyes when you are ready. You can hug each other and profess your love to each other. Leave that sacred space with the intention of staying connected, at peace, and in love with your partner.

Restoring Trust and Bringing Back the Spark

Sometimes, you and your partner lose the spark you once had. It could be because you've both been too busy to pay attention to each other, or even worse, you're struggling with the aftermath of infidelity. When it's the latter, it's tough to feel the spark or connection when you no longer trust each other. Is it possible to work through this situation and get things back to how they used to be? You can make things happen if you both want things to work out. Who better to help you navigate this ugly, rough patch in your relationship than Raphael himself?

When you no longer trust each other, Raphael's energy can mend your broken trust. He shows you how you contributed to current affairs and how you can take responsibility for fixing things. He shows you how to forgive and gives you the strength to be open-minded enough to understand each other and see through the issues beneath the surface.

More than anyone else, Raphael knows how important it is to find the spark of true love in a relationship. His efforts are all directed towards getting you in touch with your emotions and doing the same for your partner. This way, you can both remember what it was about each other that had you unable to think of much else in the first place. He guides you without judgment until you both rediscover the joy of being together again. This way, you can get back the romance you lost and feel some hope for your future.

It is possible to restore the trust that you've lost. Here is a great ritual that you can use to bring back the trust and ensure that the spark you had for each other is returned as well.

1. The first thing you must do is create a sacred space. Prepare it as you usually would, but try to make it as romantic as possible this time. You can use white and green flowers, some lovely music, preferably without lyrics, and soft, gentle lighting. Consider using

incense or oils that are reminiscent of love and softness. Rose essential oil is an excellent choice.
2. You and your partner should sit facing each other and hold each other's hands. Close your eyes and take a few grounding breaths.
3. Now that you both feel present and grounded, invoke Archangel Raphael's presence. You can each take turns asking him to infuse his healing love into your partnership. You do not have to use specific words. All that matters is you speak from your heart and sincerely.
4. You may both talk about what you've been struggling with regarding trust. Importantly, the main point of this conversation should be reminiscing about the best times you had at the start of the relationship when the spark was still strong. This is where your focus should be.
5. When you're done sharing, spend 5 minutes staring deeply into each other's eyes. You must maintain eye contact. This is not a staring contest but an opportunity to bear your souls. In the spirit of vulnerability, it is easier for Archangel Raphael's energy to flow. Don't be alarmed if either or both of you cry.
6. Profess your love for each other and your commitment to a healthy and successful relationship.
7. When you are ready, you both need to thank Archangel Raphael for his assistance and for helping you rediscover the spark you thought was lost.

Dealing with Trauma from Past Relationships

Raphael can help you work through the trauma you have faced in past relationships. If you have dealt with bad experiences from past relationships, like abuse in any form (physical, mental, emotional, financial, etc.,) betrayal, constant arguments, and so on, you're probably carrying wounds from those relationships. Those wounds will affect how you interact with your present or future partner. Your past will cause you to act in certain ways, interpret things through specific lenses, have unique emotional responses and behaviors, and so on. Logically, you know this is a new, different person. Still, you act in ways meant to keep you from getting hurt again. Sometimes, your choices aren't necessarily the best for the relationship.

Ugliness from your past can make it hard for you to bond with anyone else emotionally, as you keep a part of yourself permanently hidden – usually, the vulnerable part, which you need to share to develop a deeper connection with your partner. You find it hard to trust others, so you retreat behind a wall to avoid getting hurt, but that also keeps you from having a true, loving connection. You approach your interactions with prospective partners cautiously, which can scare them away from you. If you manage to land a relationship, you may find yourself dealing with conflicts, power imbalances, and being iced out as you repeat the patterns from the past because they're now ingrained in your mind. They're a habit.

Another insidious thing about your traumatic past is that it can cause low self-esteem. That can lead you to settle for the bare minimum. At worst, you find yourself dealing with criticism, manipulation, and emotional abuse at the hands of your new partner (who is basically the old one but with a different face). You need help working through the self-limiting beliefs if you want a shot at a healthy relationship where you can be authentic and feel safe. You want to be in a relationship where you can communicate freely without fear. But how can you do this? In addition to therapy, you can ask Raphael to help you.

The trauma that casts a shadow on your relationships can be healed, and Raphael is just the Archangel for the job. He can support you and help you regain your emotional and mental health. He does this by gently leading you to face your wounds and treat them so that you can release the pain and focus on the here and now. He can show you how to trust and be vulnerable once more so that you can return to enjoying love.

As devastating as the effects of trauma are, you can handle them with Archangel Raphael's help. You can do the following ritual to help you heal those wounds.

1. Go somewhere quiet and free from disturbances and distractions.
2. Now, light a white candle. White represents the energy of healing, just like the color green. Still, it also represents the concept of purity and innocence.
3. Lie down, or sit comfortably. Close your eyes. Take deep, grounding breaths, allowing your body and mind to be rooted in the moment.

4. In your mind's eye, imagine a brilliant, soothing emerald light surrounding you. This light comes from Archangel Raphael himself.
5. Invoke Raphael's presence by saying you need him to help you heal. Once more, the words you use for this ritual don't matter as long as you speak from your heart. Remember that your intention for this ritual is to find all the emotional wounds you may not be aware of, bring them to light, and heal them. If you remember certain traumatic experiences as you sit in Raphael's presence, feel free to share them with him. You can break down in tears or be overcome with emotions. Remember, you can share everything because you're safe with him.
6. When you feel ready, thank him for listening to you. Thank Raphael because you know that he will heal not just the trauma you are aware of but the deeper wounds you've been unable to access with your conscious mind.

The Need for Humility

When you reach out to Raphael, you cannot expect him to fix things without you putting in the work. The thing to do is ask him to share insights about how to fix the relationship issues you're facing. There's always some concrete action you can take to show your partner that you still love them and desire to make the relationship work, so listen and watch closely for any messages that come your way after reaching out to Raphael.

Also, you cannot be prideful when contacting Raphael to fix your relationship. After learning that he can help relationships, some people think they can get Raphael to force their partner to come crawling back, apologizing, and putting in all the work on their own. They don't want to have to do anything, but that's not how it works. Don't be like them. You must be humble and be willing to seek forgiveness.

You must put aside whatever notions you have about deserving reparations or anything of the sort and simply forgive your spouse (provided your issues aren't life-threatening, as in the case of abuse, for instance). You must show mercy to help Raphael be even more effective at his work.

Now that you know how Raphael can help you heal your relationships and marriages, you'll discover how you can also draw on his power to heal your body. The next chapter is all about being healed with his loving touch.

Chapter Six: Healing the Physical Body

Archangel Raphael can heal your body. It is important to note that you should not use prayer or meditation as a substitute for seeking medical help. You must understand that working with Archangel Raphael is meant to complement modern forms of treatment.

Hands-on Healing

Hands-on healing is a healing process that involves channeling the energy meant to heal your body using touch. It is about working with the spiritual connection between one and all. You see, it may look like you are separate from every other person and every other thing around you, but the truth is that everything is connected. Hands-on healing exploits this connection between you and everything else. You are connected to various energies, including healing energies. Therefore, hands-on healing is about the healer and the one to be healed working with these energies. It can help with physical, emotional, and mental well-being. You can work with the healing power of Archangel Raphael to assist you with this particular healing method. Here's how it works.

1. You must first create a sacred space where there will be no distractions and no disturbances. This is important because you do not want to disrupt the flow of healing energy between yourself and the person you will be working with. Make this space conducive for spiritual work by changing the lighting,

playing soft spiritual music without lyrics, lighting candles, lighting incense, and placing crystals around you.

2. Close your eyes, sit or lie down, and take a few deep breaths. Then, intend for Archangel Raphael to join you. You can call upon his presence by verbally asking out loud that he participate in this ritual or by asking him in your mind until you begin to feel his energy flowing in and around you.

3. When you feel ready, put your hands on whatever body part requires healing.

4. In your mind's eye, imagine your hands emanating emerald-green energy. You are working as a conduit for this energy so that Archangel Raphael can allow the light to flow into this person's body and heal them.

5. Keep your hands over the body part. You may notice the differences in temperature, energy flow, magnetism, and vibrations. You need to connect with your intuition as you perform this hands-on healing exercise because it is a very intuitive process.

6. You may receive special messages or insights from Archangel Raphael. Use them to better channel the energy you're working with. For instance, you may realize that the pain you're focused on comes from somewhere else. Raphael might make you inclined to place your hands elsewhere other than where the pain is. This

7. As you continue to work on the body part, you must adopt an attitude of love. Make sure your heart chakra is overflowing with love. Remember, healing is actually rooted in love. So, connect with divinity from a place of love and understand that.

8. When you sense that the session is complete, thank Raphael for being present and offering his help. Tell him that you trust that he will pick up from where you left off and that the healing is already done, even if it doesn't appear that way now. Thank him for offering guidance, insight, love, and energy to transform the body into its original, healthy form. When you are ready, take a last deep, grounding breath, and then gradually let go of your intentions. Trust that Archangel Raphael is on the job.

Gem Water Healing

Did you know you could work with Archangel Raphael's energy and gem water to heal yourself or someone else? Gem water is an elixir made by energetically charging some water with gems. This water can be consumed and applied to the body. It creates the physical reaction and healing that you seek. The water takes on the energetic healing properties of whichever gem you put into it.

Gem water is an elixir that is charged with Raphael's energy for healing.
https://pxhere.com/en/photo/910362

When you want to work with gem water, you first must figure out what each one is meant to do. Next, ensure that the ones you choose are safe to put in water.

It is important to understand that every gem has a unique energy signature. You don't want to use a gemstone meant to help with digestion to stop a headache. It's not like it wouldn't work. It would be more expedient to go with the more effective option. Here are some gems and what you can use them for:

- **Amethyst** is excellent for alertness, brain, nerves, lungs, intersectional tract, low blood pressure, swellings, bruises, tension release, and pain.
- **Blue apatite** is excellent for healing bone fractures and osteoporosis, improving appetite, and building stronger teeth and healthier joints.

- **Citrine** is excellent for the stomach, digestion, pancreas, and spleen.
- **Dolomite** is a good one to use for pain. It will help you with cramping, metabolic imbalances, heart issues, circulation problems, and cleaning out your blood vessels.
- **Emerald** is excellent for your eyes, gallbladder, heart, and respiratory system. You can also use it to battle inflammation and infections.
- **Green beryl** can eliminate pollutants and toxins. It is excellent for the thyroid gland, bladder, kidney, and autoimmune issues. You can also use this to deal with allergies.
- **Hematite** can be used to improve circulation.
- **Indigolite or blue tourmaline** – both are excellent when it comes to dealing with burns, joint issues, and numbness.
- **Jasper** helps the body feel stronger and more energized thanks to its effects on circulation and temperature regulation.
- **Kabamba** can be used to deal with internal organ inflammation, cases of flu, and colds.
- Use **labradorite** to regulate the menstrual and hormonal cycles.
- **Molokaite** can relieve nausea and constipation and help intestinal health. It is also excellent for healing wounds and boosting the immune system.
- **Nephrite** can detoxify the body, help ear issues, and improve balance.
- **Onyx** can be used for more efficient waste elimination, a stronger immune system, and better hearing.
- **Peridot** can help you deal with detoxification, burning fat, and eliminating warts and fungal infections.
- **Clear quartz** is amazing for healthy nails, hair, and skin. It can also help your nerves, brain, hormones, water balance, and the glands in your body. On top of that, you can use it to amplify the effects of other crystals.
- **Rose quartz** can be used to deal with sexual problems.
- **Smoky quartz** can help with intestinal issues, inflammation, pain in the body, and a weak immune system. You can also use it to improve your nerve health and handle the effects of radiation.

- **Turquoise** is excellent for heartburn, ear infections, and respiratory diseases. If you're dealing with cramps and inflammation, this is an excellent crystal to create your gem water.
- **Green tourmaline** or **verdelite** are excellent for all nervous conditions, detoxification, the reduction of scarring, and better intestinal health.
- **Zoisite** can reduce stress and inflammation.

Creating Healing Gem Water

Now that you know the appropriate gemstones to use, it is time to move on to the process of creating your gem water for healing.

1. Before anything else, you need to cleanse the gemstones and then charge them with your intention. You must put them under the moonlight or in sunlight to cleanse them. You can also bury them in the earth for a night, or you may simply sit with them and use some salt to rubble over them and get rid of the other energies from other people and places that may not serve your purpose. You need to cleanse your gemstones because, in the handling process, other people have touched them and left behind their energies on them. Sometimes, these energies are not necessarily good for you.
2. You now need to charge them with your energy. You will also be infusing these stones with the energy of Archangel Raphael. To do this, sit with them in your hands or around you and close your eyes. Take a few grounding breaths, and then in your mind's eye, envision Archangel Raphael's powerful emerald green light coming down from the sky and going into each crystal to charge it. Imagine that each crystal now has a distinct, green luminosity around it. You have now charged these crystals or the healing power of Archangel Raphael.
3. Prepare your gem water. All you have to do is put the crystals into a glass container filled with water.
4. Enlist Archangel Raphael's help. All you have to do is call on Raphael and ask him to charge the water with his healing power, much like he "troubled" the pool at Bethesda so that people could jump in and get healed. In your mind's eye, see more of his healing green energy infusing into the water from the crystals

so it glows with a beautiful emerald green.
5. As you sit with the gem water, be clear about your intentions. You can state them out loud or just ponder them in your mind.
6. Drink or apply the water to the problematic area. When you're drinking gem water, take time to focus on the fact that you are seeking healing. Trust that you will inevitably receive it. This makes it easier for the gem water to flow through you and correct any energetic imbalances. As you drink, envision the green light flowing down your throat and radiating to every part of your body.
7. You can also use your gem water for other things like watering your plants, bathing, misting your skin, etc.
8. When you're done creating, you should thank Archangel Raphael for giving you the energy that will heal you and anyone else using that water.

Crystal Mojo Bags

A mojo bag is a little pouch with special items like crystals, charms, stones, personal effects, herbs, and spices. All of the things in the mojo bag have their own energetic influence, which, when combined together, give you specific results. Since this book is about Archangel Raphael and healing, it will cover healing mojo bags. Sometimes, people call the mojo bag a gris-gris, conjure, or root bag.

There is no wrong or right way to make a mojo bag. So, do not let anyone make you feel like you're not using it right. Consider the instructions in this book as guidelines on what you can do, and go with your intuition if you feel like getting creative. In this case, you are making a crystal mojo bag, so whatever you do, put a crystal in it that will help you accomplish your healing intention. Think of these bags as talismans. You can have the energy of this talisman upon you and around you at all times just by carrying it wherever you go.

When working with these bags to heal yourself or the people around you, you can invoke Archangel Raphael to infuse them with his healing energy. He can also help you choose the right crystal for the job. All you need to do is sit, ground yourself, hold each crystal one at a time, and pay attention to any intuitive nudge you receive from Raphael. Here are instructions for how you can create your own crystal mojo bags.

1. Begin by setting your intention for the bag you'd like to create. In this case, your intention is for healing. Be clear about the sort of healing that you seek from this mojo bag, whether it be physical, mental, emotional, or spiritual. Invoke Archangel Raphael at this point so he can supercharge your intention.
2. Pick your crystals. Choose the one that you sense goes well with Archangel Raphael's energy. Do not rush this process. You shouldn't work with a crystal if you feel unsure about it. Some of the crystals you can work with include clear quartz, rose quartz, malachite, green aventurine, and green emerald.
3. Get the materials you need to create your mojo bag. You'll need a small bit of white or green fabric or a white or green pouch. You'll also need the crystals you chose, a pen, and paper. You can add things that mean something to you or the person you're trying to heal. Herbs and spices that represent the idea of healing to you are fine, too.
4. Prepare the bag. Close your eyes and take some deep, long breaths to ground yourself. In your mind's eye, see Raphael's light coming down from the sky and engulfing you completely. Imagine that this light surrounds all the materials you'll use to create the crystal mojo bag. Feel your hands flowing and pulsing with Raphael's energy. Take a moment to thank Archangel Raphael for giving you his power and assistance.
5. You must cleanse the crystals if you haven't already and then charge them with your intention.
6. As you put them in the bag, say an affirmation about what you want them to do. There is no specific way to state your affirmation. Just make sure that you acknowledge that it is already a done deal. You can also affirm that Raphael's energy charges each crystal and other materials.
7. This step is the personalization process. This is the part where you put personal items in the bag. You can also add other materials that correspond energetically to your intention. You need to take the pen and paper and write down your intentions, then fold that paper neatly and place it in the bag.
8. Now that you've put all the materials you want in the bag, it is time to seal it with Archangel Raphael's energy. Imagine that the green light circles the bag, powerfully radiating around it, as you

seal the bag or tie a security using a string.

9. Once more, call upon Archangel Raphael and tell him what you want the bag to do. Thank him for his assistance as you witness his emerald light working its magic.

10. You can place the bag somewhere safe and sacred. Alternatively, you can carry it around to enjoy its effects all day. You can also leave it under your pillow.

11. It will be necessary to recharge the bag with energy every now and then. Hold it in your hands and invoke Archangel Raphael's presence. State that you want the bag to be recharged with this energy, visualize the emerald green light charging it, and then you're good to go again. If you want to edit your written intention, you can do that before you recharge the bag.

Healing Visualization

Raphael can also help you heal by using visualization. You're already familiar with this, as most of the meditations and rituals here require you to be able to visualize his emerald green light. Visualization is a powerful technique that should never be overlooked. With this particular technique, you will imagine that your body has already received the healing you seek. By placing this in the past, you make it inevitable for your body, mind, and soul to come into alignment with the fact that you have already seen yourself as healed. If you place your healing in the future, the odds of it happening will be slim because it'll always be in the future. Every time tomorrow rolls around, it never does because it becomes today. In other words, the only time is now. By putting something in the past, you ensure that you encourage your subconscious mind to accept that it is already a done deal, making it easier for Archangel Raphael's energies to flow through you and heal you. Here's the process that you need to follow to use visualization to receive your healing:

1. Find somewhere nice and comfortable where you will not be distracted or bothered. Wear comfortable clothing to sit or lie down with ease. Choose a position you can maintain for 10 to 15 minutes.

2. Close your eyes, part your lip slightly, and take a few deep, grounding breaths in through your nose and out of your slightly parted lips. You may notice that the exhales are longer than your

inhales. If that's the case, this is fine. If it helps, you can play soothing meditation music to help you focus on the moment. Essential oils can also create the spiritual ambiance required for visualization.

3. Reach out to Archangel Raphael. You can mentally repeat his name over and over until you begin to feel his energy welling up within and around you. Alternatively, you could say, *"Archangel Raphael, I seek your presence. I desire your help. Please come to me right now."* And then, you wait until you begin to feel him unmistakably.

4. Once you sense that you have invoked Raphael, it is time to envision your body healing. For instance, assume you're trying to heal a sprain in your ankle that keeps you from walking properly. In this case, imagine yourself running or walking confidently and powerfully. Imagine yourself walking as though your ankle never hurt a day in your life. Note that you must be in your body during this visualization exercise. In other words, do not look at yourself walking or running as if you are watching yourself in a movie. Instead, take the place of the actor. You should feel each step as you hit the pavement with each foot. You shouldn't be able to see your face; you should only see the parts of your body you would see were you to get up and walk.

5. Use all your senses to take this visualization exercise up a notch. In this example, feel the vibrations reverberating through your body as each foot hits the pavement. You must hear the sounds around you as you walk and notice your breathing as you walk. Using all your imaginative senses will make this feel so real that what feels like some point and time in the future actually feels like it's happening here and now. You'll know you've done this correctly because, by the time you come out of the visualization, you will be shocked to discover that you are still sitting in your room.

6. As you continue to walk in your imagination, envision this emerald healing light of Archangel Raphael flowing around the problematic area of your body.

7. When you feel ready, gradually return your awareness to the room you're in. Before you open your eyes, affirm that your body has been healed and the changes you seek have been

implemented. You may sit in the feeling of being healed for as long as you like, and when you're ready, thank Archangel Raphael for his assistance and open your eyes.

Prayers and Meditation

The subjects of prayer meditation to connect to Archangel Raphael have already been discussed in Chapter 2. However, no details were given on how to ask for his healing. Whether you have chosen to pray to Archangel Raphael or to meditate until you feel his presence, asking him to heal your body is not complicated. If you have chosen the prayer route, you must communicate your desires sincerely.

If you are using meditation to seek healing, all you have to do is bring awareness to the part of your body that requires it. Then, in your mind, envision Archangel Raphael's healing emerald green energy flowing through and around that body part until you feel like the exercise should be brought to a close. At this point, offer your thanks to Archangel Raphael. You can repeat your prayers or meditations as often as you'd like. In addition, it would be helpful to constantly remind yourself whenever you feel like the pain or issue isn't going away. After you do, you must have faith that it is being handled.

In the next chapter, you'll be learning about angelic Reiki. You'll discover how you can work with it to attain whatever you need from Raphael.

Chapter Seven: Angelic Reiki

Angelic Reiki is powered by angels who generously offer their guidance and assistance. It involves energy realignment and healing in all ways, physically, emotionally, and mentally. This practice is about developing a stronger connection to angelic dimensions where the Archangels can be found. The difference between traditional Reiki and angelic Reiki is that the angelic version is of a higher dimensional vibration.

Angelic reiki is powered by the angels.
https://unsplash.com/photos/r6_xcsNg0kw

The Origin of Angelic Reiki

Angelic Reiki was taught to Kevin Core (a Reiki Master) by the Archangel Metatron around 2002, and in 2008, Christine Core took over from Kevin. With Archangel Raphael's guidance and Reiki, you can affect the structure of cells in the body and molecules in everything around you. You can expect changes to occur that will restore harmony and balance to you on an energetic level, and these changes will ripple outward to positively affect your body and life. Angelic Reiki allows you to create a clear route for divine powers to flow freely toward you, especially as you work with the various symbols.

On Attunements

When it comes to angelic Reiki, you'll need to experience various attunements so that you can open up your chakras or energy centers even more, making it easier for you to work with healing energy and to remain in vibrational alignment with the angels as you do your work. You can think of the attunement as an initiation on a cosmic level, granting you access to higher energies. It's a way to become a free-flowing conduit for divinity to act through so you can heal others around you, and when needed, you can heal yourself too. To experience attunement, it's best to work with a Reiki Teacher or Master because you cannot do this alone. These people have years of experience and have been under the tutelage of other Masters, so it only makes sense to make things easier for yourself by letting them help you.

What can you expect to happen during an attunement? The Master will use various methods to harmonize the Reiki frequencies in your energy system. You'll have to work with meditation and specific rituals and experience the direct transmission of divine energy. There's no set way to experience these things because every human has a different energy foundation, and everyone is at different stages when it comes to being prepared for attunement. One thing you can be certain of is that you will be profoundly moved during the process. Your energy blockages will be cleared, and your chakras will be properly aligned for the first time in your life. You'll awaken to the fullness of who you are and discover latent healing powers within you that you can channel as needed.

Before you get a Reiki attunement, look into getting a Reiki Master with a good reputation. Not only should others be able to vouch for their abilities, but you should also be able to align with them easily. Trust is an integral part of the process of attunement. When you've found a great Master, connect with them, and let them know you'd love their assistance with attunement, and they'll let you know what to expect, what you require, and what you'll need to pay. It's best to get all this out of the way before you proceed. Also, you need to be certain that this is something you want because you cannot afford to take it lightly. This is the gateway you will step through to become a powerful healer. Combining this with consciously working with Archangel Raphael's power will make you an unstoppable healing force.

Angelic Reiki Healing Techniques

You'll need to work with certain techniques for this healing modality. One technique involves hand placements, where you must place your hand in certain positions to allow proper energy flow. Your hands may be directly on the body, or they may only hover non - intrusively. Still, they have to match up to the energy centers and channels on the body so that Raphael's angelic healing power can flow and do its thing. Every placement is precise and has a specific role. If you place your hands on or around the crown chakra, for instance, it will help you to feel connected to the spirit realm, clear your mind, and relax. When on the heart energy center, you encourage healing (especially of the emotions), compassion, and deep love. It's also fine to place your hands right over the part of the body experiencing discomfort.

Another technique involves symbols and visualization. You work with specific symbols to draw the divine energy you need to heal yourself or another and use specific visualization exercises to help. The symbols serve as amplifiers of energies and vibrations that facilitate specific intentions. They pull the energy of celestial beings to lend you assistance. When you focus on the visualizations and symbols, and you and the person you're healing intend what you want to accomplish, you make it easier for the healing energy to flow through your hands and create the changes you seek.

The Connection between Raphael and Reiki

Reiki practitioners understand that they are meant to be a channel of the energy Raphael brings. By understanding this, they can get out of the way and not adversely influence the healing process. Raphael can do his work by offering intuitive insight and guidance to the Reiki practitioner and the person to be healed. He helps by revealing the root of the trauma or imbalance causing distress, which is how true healing can be achieved. Usually, the Reiki Master doesn't just work with Raphael alone but with other angelic entities. Think of them as a team of Angelic EMTs, if you will. They can work with ascended masters, other angels, and other beings who specialize in healing certain things to bring you better results. Now it's time to take a look at the various Reiki symbols you can work with.

Cho Ku Rei

Cho Ku Rei for protection and cleansing.
Stephen Buck The Reiki Sangha, CC BY-SA 2.0 <https://creativecommons.org/licenses/by-sa/2.0>, via Wikimedia Commons https://commons.wikimedia.org/wiki/File:Chokurei.jpg

Cho Ku Rei is the symbol you use to cleanse and protect, and you can turn it on by drawing it on your palms when you're healing yourself or someone else. You can also draw this symbol on any energy chakra or all of them to increase energy flow, and little wonder, because it's known as the symbol of power. It is said that "Cho Ku Rei" literally translates to

"Channel all the Universe's power here and now." Think of this symbol as a prerequisite before you begin your Reiki practice. Like the quartz crystal to other crystals, Cho Ku Rei amplifies the energy of the other Reiki symbols.

How to Draw Cho Ku Rei

1. To draw this symbol, draw a line from left to right, then down so it forms an upside-down L.
2. Draw a spiral to the right at the bottom of that L. The outermost part of the spiral should be close to the first horizontal line.
3. Keep drawing the spiral from the outside to the inside until you have three spiraling lines. Do not lift your pen until you connect it to the vertical line in the middle with the smallest spiral.

The horizontal line of this symbol is the connection you're establishing with universal energies. The vertical line is the flow of powerful light from the soul star chakra into all the other centers and channels in the body before terminating in the root chakra. The spiral you draw should create seven intersections with the vertical line, representing the seven major chakras. You must use the same precise directions, no matter which hand you choose. In other words, don't reverse it when you change hands. You can draw this on the main seven chakras (crown, third eye, throat, heart, solar plexus, sacral, and root chakras) and the secondary chakras (feet, knees, hips, shoulders, ears, and eyes). You can also draw on the main organs and on the front and back of the body to ensure protection.

This symbol is excellent for stimulating all your energy centers, fighting fatigue, improving your mood, protecting your energy and physical bodies, removing blocks and bad energies, and so on. You can maximize its power by visualizing Archangel Raphael's green light emanating from the symbol as you draw it.

Sei He Ki

Sei He Ki for harmony.

L orlando, CC BY-SA 4.0 <https://creativecommons.org/licenses/by-sa/4.0>, via Wikimedia Commons https://commons.wikimedia.org/wiki/File:Sei_He_Ki.jpg

Sei He Ki is a powerful symbol that brings you harmony, balances your emotions, and heals them. Like the previous symbol, you can activate this one on your chakras and palms. It cleanses and promotes the flow of spiritual energy.

How to Draw Sei He Ki

1. First, draw a line slanted at a 45-degree angle from right to left to draw this symbol.
2. Draw from right to left without lifting your hand to have a slanted letter V.
3. Next, draw from right to left again to have a mirrored N.
4. Draw a short vertical line, and draw a curved line at the bottom with the curve leaning right. When you're done, it should look like you have a slanted letter V with the number 5 at the bottom. This is the first part. You can lift your hand off the paper to draw the next part.

5. Next, you must draw a very short horizontal line above the slanted V, starting from the halfway point and terminating at the top end of the V.
6. Without lifting your hand, draw a larger semicircle encompassing the first sign and the number 5.
7. Lift your hand off the paper, and draw two arches on the larger semicircle beneath the slanted V. The second arch should be higher than the first. When you're done, it should look like you have a small letter m on the larger semicircle.

This symbol will help you connect with divinity so you can easily figure out emotional problems tucked away in your subconscious. You can use it when there's conflict, not by drawing it on the people but discreetly on various areas of the room. This way, the tense environment can be flooded with calmness and peace. You can also use this symbol to assist with addictions and stop intrusive and negative thoughts in their tracks. Use it when you or someone else feels stressed. If it helps, consider Sei He Ki as the window you open when everywhere else feels energetically stuffy.

Hon Sha Ze Sho Nen

Hon Sha Ze Sho Nen for healing.
Stephen Buck The Reiki Sangha, CC BY-SA 4.0 <https://creativecommons.org/licenses/by-sa/4.0>, via Wikimedia Commons
https://commons.wikimedia.org/wiki/File:Honshazeshonen.jpg

This symbol is excellent for healing at a distance. It means "Without past, present, or future." Use this symbol to help you channel Archangel Raphael's healing energy across time and space so that they will receive their miracle no matter where the subject to be healed is. This symbol also transcends time, as you can send it to work on your past, present, or future.

How to Draw Hon Sha Ze Sho Nen

This one will take a bit of practice to master drawing, but you can.

1. First, draw a line from right to left.
2. Draw a line from top to bottom that intersects your horizontal line. You should now have a cross.
3. Imagine there's a circle around the cross. Draw a line from the midpoint of the intersecting lines to the 7 o'clock point.
4. Next, draw a line from the middle of the intersecting lines to the 5 o'clock point.
5. Draw a line from left to right, close to the bottom of the vertical line. Neither point should touch the 7 or 5 o'clock line.
6. Draw a horizontal line from left to right underneath the symbol you've just drawn from steps one through five. Let the line be long enough to act as a table for the top symbol.
7. Next, place your pen or finger on the right side of the 6th line, just above it, so it almost touches the 5 o'clock point of the line from step four. Then draw a line that slants at a 45-degree angle, crossing down through the line from step six and not going beyond the starting point of that line.
8. Draw a short vertical line to the right beneath the seventh line.
9. From the top of the vertical line from the previous step, draw a short horizontal line to the right.
10. Now, draw a short line from the endpoint of the previous one downward. If you've done this right, you should have a small, three-sided box with no bottom.
11. Draw a very short horizontal line inside the box from left to right.
12. Underneath the drawing you now have, draw a horizontal line that slants subtly upwards from left to right. Think of it as a table carrying the other signs.

13. Draw another line beneath that starts from the middle of line twelve and slants subtly upward but stops just before the end of line twelve.
14. Draw a vertical line from top to bottom from the middle of line twelve. If you've done this right, you should have what looks like an F.
15. To the left of this "F," draw a vertical line from top to bottom that slants subtly to the right and ends below the bottom of line fourteen.
16. Beneath all the previous drawings, start from the middle and draw a slight curve down and out to the left.
17. Return to the start of line sixteen, and draw another line that curves slightly down and out to the right. If you've done this right, it should look like the roof of a house.
18. Draw a short horizontal line from left to right underneath this roof.
19. Underneath the roof that houses a short horizontal line, start from the end, and draw a horizontal line from left to right, and then without lifting your hand, draw a line down that curves to the left as if it's part of a circle. Let it stop underneath the start of this line so you have what looks like a shark fin.
20. Draw a line that curves down and to the right next to line nineteen.
21. Within the curved line twenty, draw another smaller line that curves down and to the right and is encompassed in line twenty.
22. Finally, draw a line that starts slightly above line twenty but goes down and curves to the left, terminating slightly below the end of line 20.

You can merge Cho Ku Rei, Sei He Ki, and Hon Sha Ze Sho Nen together to allow an even more powerful flow of energy from Raphael to work on your intention.

Working with Reiki and Raphael

1. Go somewhere quiet and conducive for energy work. There should also be no distractions or disturbances.

2. Set your intention for healing, whether for yourself, a loved one, or even a pet.
3. Sit comfortably, close your eyes, and take a few centering breaths while keeping your awareness on your heart chakra.
4. Now, out loud or in your mind, call on Archangel Raphael, and ask him to facilitate the healing process.
5. Open your eyes, and activate the Reiki symbols on your palms, beginning with Cho Ku Rei.
6. Place your hands on the part of the body that needs healing, or you may just let them hover. Suppose the person you want to heal isn't present. In that case, you can activate the Hon Sha Ze Sho Nen Reiki symbol and hold your hands over their photo or some other personal effect.
7. Allow your hands to move where your intuition guides them, envisioning that they burn with Raphael's brilliant, bright emerald green light as you work.
8. While letting the energy flow, you can use healing affirmations in your mind or say them out loud. Continue with this, and let your intuition guide you.
9. When you feel ready, end the session by thanking Archangel Raphael, and then let your energy connection to the angelic realm go.
10. Ground yourself by imagining roots connecting your feet to the earth's core.

Reiki Principles

Reiki has certain guidelines or ethics you should follow to get the best of it. These principles are a strong foundation that makes you more efficient at using your abilities for good. These are the principles, all of them worth remembering.

"For now, I choose not to be angry." Anger is a disruptive force that can cause energy to flow out of alignment, making it hard to experience healing. This emotion must be released by both the Reiki master and the patient receiving treatment. Anger is so powerful that it will cause an imbalance spiritually, mentally, and emotionally. This makes it tough for the healer's touch to channel the healing energy freely to the recipient and tougher still for the recipient to accept the healing power trying to flow through him. So, choosing not to be angry implies you will remain peaceful, calm, and in control of your emotions. It means you recognize where your anger is coming from, but you choose to master it rather than let it consume you. You choose to feel it and then release it. You could do this using breathwork, meditation, journaling, or whatever method feels right.

"For now, I choose not to worry." Worry also does you no good when you're working with Reiki. It is far better to ensure your mind is in the here and now rather than being anxious about a future that may not play out how you fear it will. Worry is natural, sure . . . but too much of it, and you will wreak havoc on your emotions and your mind. In Reiki, everyone working with energy must be present, as healing comes here and now, not later. You worry when you're afraid and untrusting, not sure that life will work out exactly as it should and that everything will be okay. If this is a habit, it will serve you to quit it. Reiki invites you to trust in the universe and its intelligence. Nothing happens that isn't by divine design. When you know this, you no longer feel the need to know what comes next or to control results. You can just focus on living from one moment to the next, which is excellent for encouraging healing.

"For now, I choose to be grateful." Gratitude is a conscious choice to be thankful for all the good in your life. In the attitude of gratitude, you open your eyes to the many blessings and gifts that you get to experience every day. You are thankful because you know there's always something good to be appreciated if you're willing to see it. Practicing gratitude is an excellent way to encourage positive energy flow in every aspect of your life. It's about moving your attention away from what your ego considers "bad" to the abundance of good in your life. This positive energy is necessary for allowing Reiki energy to flow freely and heal you or another. It's also a good idea to express gratitude for the power of Reiki, as this dramatically intensifies the effects of the Reiki master's work.

"For now, I choose honesty." This means that you choose to be transparent and truthful in all your ways. It's about understanding the need for congruence in what you intend, what you actually do, and what you say. It's about ensuring you're never deceiving anyone, not even yourself. In other words, if there are things you must do or changes you must make that would benefit your health and well-being, it's best to face the truth and do something about it. The energy flow will be even more beneficial when you choose to be honest with yourself and work with the truth of your situation rather than pretend it isn't there. As for the Reiki practitioner, he must also practice honesty. He must be upfront with you about the extent of his experience and what you should expect from your sessions with him so that you have the power to make decisions based on accurate information.

"For now, I choose kindness." Kindness is the final cornerstone of Reiki. You must respect all life by demonstrating kindness, compassion, and empathy. Everything that lives deserves compassion and carries undeniable value. It doesn't matter how they look or where they are in life. Reiki masters know it is important to honor the spark of divinity and the breath of life in all things. They know that they must always be about helping people suffer less and heal better. In Reiki, being kind to yourself is also important. Self-compassion is a prerequisite to compassion for others because you cannot give what you don't have. Being kind to yourself means setting clear boundaries, doing what you must to stay healthy, and remaining in harmony as often as possible. Kindness also extends to all other creatures, not just humans. The environment deserves kindness, too. By making this a principle to live by, you make it easier for the healing energy of Reiki to do its work in your life.

Remember that these principles aren't rules per se but are meant to help you work with Reiki more efficiently. You can interpret and embody them in whatever way is most authentic to you. As you do so, you'll experience amazing transformation and growth in your life. Now that you know how to heal others with Archangel Raphael's help, what about healing yourself? In the next chapter, you will learn about healing for healers.

Chapter Eight: Healing for Healers

Did you know that Archangel Raphael is the protector and healer of healers? Archangel Raphael is a powerful being who acts as a guardian and supports the people working in the healing arts and medical profession. He is there to offer healing energy, serve as a guide, and assist the healers. So, if you're a doctor, a nurse, or practice Reiki or any of the other healing arts, you can turn to him for help. Usually, during healing, some challenging situations can pop up. When you are faced with something you don't know how to handle, you can ask for his help and know that he will show up.

Challenges Healers Face

If you work in the healing profession, it's not an easy thing, and you should be commended for your selfless service. You must contend with challenges and obstacles along the way. Some of these challenges you may never have witnessed before, or you may be left feeling perplexed about, because, despite your best efforts, your patient is not improving. Here are some challenges you may face while helping others recover.

- **Being physically drained:** This is a real challenge because helping others heal implies you will be expending energy. This energy is not just physical but emotional and spiritual as well. When constantly tending to other people's needs, it is only natural to feel fatigued, exhausted, and, in the worst cases, burned out. This is because you must work long hours and do your best to keep your energy up and light because the unwell person also depends on that to get better. It also doesn't help that sometimes you will face illnesses that appear to be incurable, which can take a toll on your mental health. Sometimes, the illnesses are contagious, and you are at huge risk of contracting them.

- **Being emotionally burnt out:** This is another very real situation that you must face as a healer. You wake up daily and must deal with other people's suffering and pain. Naturally, no one who's going through pain feels great. The emotions are usually in lower vibrations. If you do not know how to take care of your emotional needs, it only makes sense that you will eventually take on your patients' feelings. The problem is that when this happens, you cannot give them the best care because, as mentioned before, part of healing is maintaining a positive, light outlook. When you feel emotionally drained, it affects your own emotional well-being. It makes it difficult to stay resilient in the face of the ugliest of situations.
- **Struggles with self-care and maintaining boundaries:** As a healer, you need to take care of yourself. You can't be in poor health and expect to give your best to someone struggling. It is akin to hanging off of a ledge with someone else and expecting to be able to pull them up when you're also hanging. As a healer, you need to establish clear, healthy boundaries. This is the only way you can truly serve others; therefore, you must find a way to balance your passion for helping others with your desire to care for yourself. This is not an easy thing to do. Still, fortunately, you can call on a certain celestial being whose specialty is assisting those who work as healers.
- **Finding a balance between work and personal life** is another thing you will have to face as a healer. How do you balance your work and your personal life? You are in an extremely demanding profession. Your hours tend to be long and grueling, your schedules anything but regular, and you constantly need to keep yourself open and available in case there's an emergency where you're needed. All of this makes it incredibly difficult for you to give a good amount of attention to the personal relationships you have in your life and other

aspirations you may want to fulfill.

- **Emotional resilience:** Part of your job is withstanding the barrage of emotions that would rock anyone else if they had to deal with what you do. You must find ways to handle the challenges that come your way. You will naturally find that stress is just around the corner, waiting to sink its tentacles into your mind and body. Not only that, but you also do a lot of emotional heavy lifting. You not only have to handle your emotions and ensure they're in check, but you also have to help your patients so they do not feel overwhelmed or hopeless about their situations. Therefore, you need to be able to find healthy ways to express and deal with your emotions. Otherwise, you are handling too much emotional stress, which could burn you out to the point where you are no longer useful to anyone and can't even help yourself. These are just some of the challenges that healers face in their profession. Fortunately, there are rituals, meditations, and prayers you can use to help you take care of your emotional, physical, and spiritual health so that you can help others get back to a hundred percent.

Blessed by Green Light Ritual

For this ritual, you will need a green candle, emerald crystal, and a few drops of eucalyptus oil.

Steps:
1. First, ensure you're somewhere quiet and will not be bothered or disturbed for 10 to 15 minutes.
2. Set the green candle on a safe surface before you and light it. Use a candle holder if you have one.
3. Close your eyes and take a few deep, grounding breaths. You should have the emerald crystal in your hands as you breathe.
4. In your mind's eye, imagine that a vibrant green light surrounds you, flowing from the crystal, the candle, and the sky above you. Feel the energy of this light as it wraps itself around you.
5. It is time to affirm that you are protected while healing others. You can say, *"Archangel Raphael, I trust you to keep me safe as I heal others."*

6. Place a drop of eucalyptus oil on your palms and rub them together. Take a whiff of the scent, envisioning streaks of green light going in through your nostrils into your lungs and spreading out to every bit of your body and soul.
7. Gently bring the crystal up to your heart chakra, and feel their energies merge.
8. Sit for a few minutes and be grateful, trusting that Archangel Raphael will keep you safe throughout your day as you heal others. When you are ready, open your eyes.

Shielding Ritual

For this ritual, you will need palo santo or white sage, a small bowl, and a feather.

Steps:
1. Go to your sacred space and ensure it's free of distractions and disturbances.
2. Light the palo santo or sage, and set it on a heatproof incense burner with a handle. Let it burn, allowing the smoke to move up to the ceiling.
3. With the feather and one hand, fan the smoke so that it moves around your body. If it helps, you can move the incense burner around as you fan the smoke towards you to cleanse your aura. You should move from the top of your head down towards your feet. Be careful when you do this.
4. Imagine the smoke cleansing your auric field so that anything that you've taken on from your work throughout the day is removed from you. Alternatively, you can do this ritual before you go to work. In that case, imagine instead that the smoke is fortifying your aura, keeping it safe, creating a shield that prevents you from taking on other energies and emotions that aren't pure and would bring you down.
5. Now, place the feather into the bowl. That means you have successfully created your auric shield and cleansed your aura.
6. Tell Raphael you would like him to protect you as you do your work and keep your aura as pure as possible. You can repeat this until you start to feel a shift in the energy, indicating that he has heard you.

7. When you are ready, thank Raphael for cleansing and protecting you by setting up your shield. Trust that he has heard you and will do all that you have passed.

The Healing Grid

For this ritual, you will need a set of healing crystals. You can choose clear quartz, rose quartz, amethyst, and emerald. You don't have to use all of them, but you can use a combination. You'll also need an altar or a cloth and a quiet space.

Steps:
1. Set the crystals on your altar or a cloth in your sacred space. Arrange them in a way to form a grid.
2. Pick the largest of your crystals, and let that represent Archangel Raphael himself. This crystal should go in the middle of your grid.
3. Stand before your grid or sit comfortably if you prefer. Close your eyes, part your lips slightly, and take a few centering breaths to bring you into the present moment.
4. In your mind, see healing energy that flows from Archangel Raphael into the crystal you've set in the middle of your grid.
5. Once this crystal in the middle is fully charged with Raphael's emerald energy, see the energy flow to the other crystals in the grid.
6. It is now time to pray to Raphael. Ask him to support you as you go about your healing work. Tell him to guide you whenever you feel lost about what to do to help a patient. Also, ask him to heal you as you inevitably pick up other energies that may bring you down or affect you somehow.
7. Sit in silent meditation with your grid. In your mind's eye, imagine that all the crystals are now connected with an emerald light. This light burns brighter and brighter, then beams directly into your heart chakra. From there, it radiates outwards, spreading into your palms. Feel the energy as it burns in your palms and moves from there to the rest of your body.
8. Thank Raphael for helping you. As the crystals also have their own consciousness, you should thank them for participating in this ritual and assisting you in your good work.

9. When you are ready, open your eyes and return to the present moment. You may now take apart your crystal grid and then cleanse the stones to be ready for use the next time you set up a grid.

The Healer's Prayer

"Dearest Raphael, you are the true healer.
You are my helper; you are my guide.
I seek now your power pure,
Your wisdom, strength, and all your cures.
I asked that you keep me safe,
And in your healing light, I bathe.
Keep me strong and healthy in mind and body,
That your love and grace I may embody.
Through these hands, heal and restore,
That my patients be whole as before.
For answered prayers, I thank you,
Now help me be a vessel true."

The Shielding Prayer

"Raphael, you are power and might.
Fill me now with your beautiful light.
My hands and heart are yours,
To heal all hurts and sores.
May your green energy flow through me,
To restore, to make whole, to make healthy.
Wrap me in your wing's embrace,
So bad energy leaves no trace
Upon my body and soul, by your grace,
As I take on this healing space."

Restoration Meditation

1. Sit somewhere comfortable and quiet.
2. Close your eyes and take a few deep, grounding breaths.
3. Imagine Raphael's light all around you. On each inhale, breathe in the green light. On each exhale, breathe out all the negative, stale energies you have gathered throughout the day. Imagine this energy, stress, and tension as a blackness across your shoulders.
4. With each exhale, move the dark energy from your shoulders down into your heart center and out into the world, where it dissipates.
5. Continue to breathe this way, taking in the green light and exhaling the dark energy until it feels completely clean and clear. You no longer see any darkness hovering around you.
6. It is time to thank Archangel Raphael for relieving you of the burden and negativity you've picked up on throughout your day.
7. When you are ready and completely restored, you may come out of the meditation.

You now know how to work with Archangel Raphael so you can effectively do your job as a healer. The next chapter is about how even musicians, artists, and other creatives can work with this Archangel to improve their work and tap into a constant, endless stream of creativity and inspiration.

Chapter Nine: Creative Rituals

This final chapter is for aspiring musicians, artists, and all creative people. Did you know that Archangel Raphael is also connected to creativity? This Archangel not only heals and changes your life, but he can also help you tap into your innate creativity. You can work with him to harness your artistic energies to create work superior to anything else you've ever done before.

Creativity Heals You

The incredible thing about being creative is that you can use the opportunity to heal. As a creative person, you have an inner drive to make and create things. You're not satisfied with simply consuming other people's work. If you do not take your time to create things, it can feel really heavy for you. In fact, many people feel constantly bogged down because they do not habitually express this creativity. They do not realize they would lead much happier lives if they practiced constantly creating.

Raphael Can Inspire You

Archangel Raphael can guide you in finding the root of divine inspiration. He has a way of intuitively nudging you towards the creative ideas that lie within you, untapped and unexpressed. This Archangel can connect to the hearts and minds of various creatives like musicians, writers, artists, and many more. In fact, you can tap into the inspiration and creativity of your innate abilities and the creativity of the greats who have passed on in whatever field of creative expression. In other words, with Archangel Raphael's help, you can channel the creativity of Van

Gogh if you are a painter or Sylvia Plath if you are a writer, and so on. Raphael can act as a conduit so that you can channel their energy into your work, making it something new from something seemingly borrowed.

Eliminate Creative Blocks with Raphael

When you practice invoking Archangel Raphael before you begin any creative work, you will find yourself becoming more and more aligned with his energy, which means that sometimes, you may not even have to invoke him before you start getting a stream of creative ideas. Many can't figure out what to create because they feel uninspired. Imagine having the opposite problem, where you have many ideas and can't wait to start. If only you had enough hands or a clone! This is what Archangel Raphael can do for you.

Archangel Raphael can help release creative blocks.
https://unsplash.com/photos/yn7R3DLA-ik

So, if you've ever had to deal with creative blocks that keep you from expressing your true artistic self, you know how frustrating it can be. That can be incredibly crippling, and if you allow it to continue for long enough, it will get to a point where you feel like you can't do what you really want." You do not need to wait for things to get that bad before restoring the flow of creativity. You can work with Archangel Raphael; he is always more than happy to help you break through any barriers affecting your creativity.

Never Underestimate Rituals

One powerful way to connect with Archangel Raphael's creativity and inspiration is by using rituals. When you make rituals a part of your creative process, you draw in Raphael's energy so that it is infused into your work and drives you to think outside the box. These rituals require elements like essential oils, crystals, candles, and certain colors, all of which should align with the energies of creativity and the Archangel Raphael. As an artist, you have the right to personalize the ritual to resonate with who you are. When you do a ritual, you naturally must set an intention. The process of setting an intention acts as a magnetic force that pulls in the desires you have. In this case, you desire the ability to express yourself creatively and freely.

Teaming Up with Raphael

There's no reason for you to work on your own as an artist. You will find it most productive when you have Archangel Raphael as a partner. As an artist, you will be supported in a way no one else could match. You will feel yourself being divinely inspired. In fact, you will be directly channeling the creative work you have in mind instead of overthinking it. Working with Raphael will be as if you're receiving messages and simply expressing them through your art.

Creativity in Non-Creative Spaces

For some reason, when the subject of creativity is discussed, people only think of it as music, art, dance, etc. However, every aspect of life involves creativity. In other words, you may not think that creativity is involved in the process of, say, doing your taxes. But there's creativity in everything you do.

Whether you're trying to cook a meal or devise a solution to a problem or conflict you're dealing with, you need creativity. You can reach out to Archangel Raphael whenever you feel stumped. It is often a good practice to ask yourself how you can do the things you already do better and faster. Whenever you feel stuck answering these questions, you can easily ask Raphael and trust that you will receive an answer. Humans are here to experience life and to evolve as they do so. Evolution means finding better ways to express who you are. Therefore, creativity is an inherent part of being human, and you have the right to reach out for divine help to discover new and better ways to express your authentic, higher self.

So, do not assume that this chapter is only for artists. It's for everyone. Because, like it or not, you cannot divorce yourself from creativity. Creativity is an inherent part of you and how you express yourself on this planet. If you are curious about how to spark or enhance your inner creativity, these next few rituals will be a great place to start.

Creative Flow Ritual

The purpose of this ritual is to help you be more creative.

1. First, go into your sacred space. It should be free of disturbances and distractions for at least 10 minutes.
2. Light a green candle. This represents the creative power of Archangel Raphael.
3. Close your eyes, and take a few deep, grounding breaths. You should inhale with your nose and exhale through your mouth.
4. When you feel grounded, it's time to invoke Raphael's presence. All you have to do is say: *"Raphael, I seek your help and guidance now. Please inspire me and give life to my creativity with your power."*
5. In your mind's eye, imagine you are in outer space. Imagine that it has a dark, beautiful greenish hue. See yourself surrounded by beautiful vibrant stars, with ones shining a lovely green reminiscent of Raphael's signature color.
6. Now, imagine that all the stars around you begin to emit a powerful, beautiful green luminescent light. Let this light wrap you from head to toe. Feel it pouring in through the top of your head, flowing down to your toes. This light carries new ideas, creative innovations, and wonderful art you can express.
7. Bask in this light for as long as you'd like, allowing it to recharge you. Feel excited as you realize you will soon create fantastic work.
8. When ready, you can open your eyes and thank Archangel Raphael for lending his energy to this ritual.
9. Now, it is time for you to do your creative work, whether writing, painting, or trying to devise a solution to a problem. You need to maintain trust and expectation as you do your work because this will enable the creativity to flow even better than if you had questions about whether the ritual worked.

Creative Block Obliteration Ritual

This ritual is meant to help you eliminate the creative blocks that make it impossible to express yourself creatively.

1. First, get a piece of paper, a green marker, or a pen if you like. You are also going to need a bowl of water.
2. Make you're in your sacred space and that you will not be distracted for the next 15 minutes.
3. Close your eyes. Part your lips. Breathe in through your nose and out through your mouth.
4. When you feel grounded, open your eyes and write down how exactly you feel blocked. Write down all your concerns, including your fears about whether or not you'll be able to create anything. It is important to be as vulnerable as you can. No one else will read this, so be honest with yourself and Archangel Raphael.
5. When you've got everything written down, it is time for you to work with Raphael's light. Hold the paper with both hands and imagine that Raphael's emerald green light begins to surround you.
6. Tell Raphael that you are drawing upon his energy to help you destroy and obliterate the creative blocks that have kept you stuck for a while. It is important to tell him that you truly and completely surrender to him and trust that he will help you easily overcome your obstacles.
7. Take the paper and soak it in the water bowl. This represents that you have released those blocks and that the negative, stale energies holding you back from expressing your creativity are now gone.
8. As you watch the paper dissolve, imagine that you can see the dark cloudy energy of the blocks and that they also dissipate as the paper dissolves into pieces. In your mind's eye, see the dark energy that was once your creative block turning into emerald energy. Imagine this emerald, green energy flowing into your heart, your third eye, and crown chakras.
9. Take some time to think about how you now feel free. Accept that with time, ideas will start to flow again.

10. Thank Raphael for his help.

Sacred Inspiration Ritual

The goal behind this ritual is to allow you to connect directly with divinity to experience its inspiration. It is about connecting your essence with sacred energy.

1. In your sacred space, surround yourself with things that mean a lot to you regarding your creative work. You can also have crystals, incense, and other objects that matter to you.
2. Light a white or green candle to represent the presence and power of Archangel Raphael.
3. Close your eyes, part your lips slightly, and take a few deep, grounding breaths until you feel fully present.
4. Now, invoke Raphael's presence by saying: *"Raphael, I seek you now. Please open up your source of divine inspiration, and let it flow to me and through me. I yield my body, mind, and spirit to allow the expression of this infinite, divine, sacred creativity."*
5. Continue to breathe deeply, and in your mind's eye, imagine that a golden beam of light comes down from the sky and pierces through the top of your head right through to the soles of your feet. Allow the warm golden light to encompass you. Feel it charging and rejuvenating you. This is a light of divine inspiration that you have acts Raphael to channel through you.
6. As you sit basking in this light, open your mind to the idea of receiving divine guidance.
7. When you feel ready, open your eyes and begin to work on your creative endeavors. Allow the energy of Raphael to flow through you. Let go of the need to be perfect or express things in a particular way along. Instead, trust that you are being divinely led and that every apparent mistake is part of the divine design.
8. When you finish your work, thank Raphael for being with you.

Crafting Your Sigil

You can make your own sigil to assist you in your creative process.

1. The first thing you will do is gather your materials. You'll need markers, pens or colored pencils, a piece of paper, a green

candle, and any other thing you have that you can use, like stickers, glitter, and symbols that matter to you.
2. The next thing you must do is get your sacred space ready. As usual, it must be free from distraction so that you can focus.
3. Now, light a green candle. This candle represents Raphael's energy which is going to feel your creativity.
4. Close your eyes, part your lips slightly, take a deep breath through your nose, and exhale through your lips. Continue to breathe this way until you feel centered and calm.
5. Now, invoke Archangel Raphael. You can do this by simply stating that you would like him to show up or by repeatedly calling his name. You can chant it out loud or quietly in your mind.
6. When you sense Raphael's presence, say, *"I seek your help boosting my creativity. I would love to work with your energy to be more expressive in my art."*
7. Now, take some time and infuse your mind with your intention. Think about what it is you hope to accomplish through your creativity. Think about what you want to express using your art. And then, when you figure it out, say aloud what your intention for the sigil is. Your intention could be, "I am now a vessel for divine creativity." Or "I have an abundant stream of creative ideas."
8. You will now design the sigil. First, you must allow your intuition to guide you along the process. In other words, when you put your hand on the paper and begin to write or draw, you should trust that the symbols or shapes you are creating come from a deep, deep place within you. You are divinely inspired. As you draw, imagine emerald green light flowing from your hands into the drawing material and the drawing itself. When you're done, state your intention out loud. You could say, *"With this sigil, I now declare that I have an abundance of creative, divinely inspired ideas. This sigil serves as a reminder to me of this truth."*
9. The next step is to infuse the sigil with your energy. Place the sigil where you can see it, sit down, and stare at it as you meditate. Allow your intention to fuse with it. Imagine that the sigil glows with Raphael's beautiful emerald light. This sigil will now be what you use to manifest your artistic goals.

10. Now that you have energized your sigil, it is time to finalize it. Intend that whenever you look at your sigil, it will become activated. Intend that it will draw creativity out of you with ease and flow when it is active. If you choose, you could have this sigil laminated or framed and displayed somewhere you can see it every day. You can also make it your phone's wallpaper.
11. At the end of this ritual, you must thank Raphael for giving you his power, support, and guidance throughout the process. Thank him for the inspiration and creativity that is now yours.
12. Finally, it is time to use your sigil. You can look at it whenever you feel like you are blocked or whenever you're about to start some creative work. Whenever you look at it, all you have to do is restate your intention and visualize how you would feel after having created some magnificent work.

Conclusion

You have reached the end of this book - but this is just the start. Once you put everything you have learned into practice, your life will finally transform for the better. You have discovered the profound benefits of developing a relationship with Archangel Raphael. You've learned that he can help you with your relationships, health, or expressing your creativity.

You have learned that the Archangel Raphael is unrivaled when it comes to healing. He can restore the harmony you were born with within your body, mind, and spirit. He can bring back the balance you were used to having as a child before life began to take its toll on you.

In this book, you have learned about various healing modalities, such as working with visualization, meditation, Reiki, and crystal mojo bags. You've also learned to carry Raphael's energy everywhere you go so you never feel drained while helping others heal.

When it comes to relationships, you've discovered that this celestial being has the power to help you mend whatever is broken. As a being full of compassion and love, he can see through to the heart of whatever it is you may be struggling with regarding relationships and fix the problems causing a rift between you and your partner. Also, if you are single, this being is quite an excellent matchmaker and knows exactly who would be a great fit for you. Thanks to Raphael's support, you can go stay in the relationship, regardless of how challenging it is or the kind of trauma you're dealing with from previous ones, knowing full well that you can overcome them and achieve success with your partner.

Regarding creativity, you now know that Raphael can give you access to divine inspiration. You know there is no such thing as creative blocks when your inspiration is divine. You understand that you have unlimited creative potential, and Archangel Raphael's help is just what you need to unlock the door to the greatness you carry within, the one that you and you alone can express.

Raphael is very benevolent and can help you break through the limitations in your mind that keep you from realizing just how creative you are. You can take your creative work to the next level by working with rituals and meditations.

However, you need to understand that it's not enough for you to know how to work with Raphael. You have to take this information and put it to work. That is the only way to take advantage of Raphael's wisdom, guidance, and presence. This is how you achieve results that change your life forever. You must put what you have learned to work so that you can constantly be in alignment with Raphael's healing vibration.

When you practice engaging with Raphael daily, you will find improvements to your health beyond anything you've ever thought possible. Basically, you're going to feel like a kid again!

Finally, you need to understand that you develop your relationship with Raphael not by reading but by approaching him with sincerity and vulnerability. You will have to completely yield to him and trust that he is not only present in your life but that he is actively working to assist you in every way he knows how. All you have to do is open your heart to accept his love, guidance, and healing energy to experience a life touched by divinity.

Correspondences Sheet

The following is a sheet of correspondence that you can use whenever you are trying to come up with creative ways to interact with Archangel Raphael or craft your own meditations, prayers, and rituals.

Day of the week - Wednesday

Hour of the day - 10:00 a.m. to 11:00 a.m.

Feast - February 14, also known as the Feast of Archangel Raphael

Zodiac sign - Virgo, Gemini

Planets - Mercury, Uranus

Angel number - 3

Direction - East

Element - Air

Color - Green

Sigil - The Caduceus

Herbs, oils, plants, and trees - Peppermint, eucalyptus, chamomile, lavender, and rosemary

Crystals - Peridot, green aventurine, malachite, emerald

Metal - Copper, mercury

Animals - Deer, dove, peacock, fish

Tarot card - The Lovers

Musical note - F

Chakra - Heart

Incense - Lavender, frankincense
Planet healing - Earth
Symbolic tool - Healing staff
Astrological house - 6th house (The House of Health and Wellness)
Virtue - Compassion
Sacred geometry - Flower of Life
Metals - Platinum, silver
Season - Spring
Musical instrument - Flute, harp
Body system - Respiratory system
Gemstone essence - Rose quartz
Elemental being - Sylphs (air spirits)
Energy frequency - 528 Hz (the miracle frequency)
Prayer beads - Rose quartz beads or green aventurine beads

Here's another book by Mari Silva that you might like

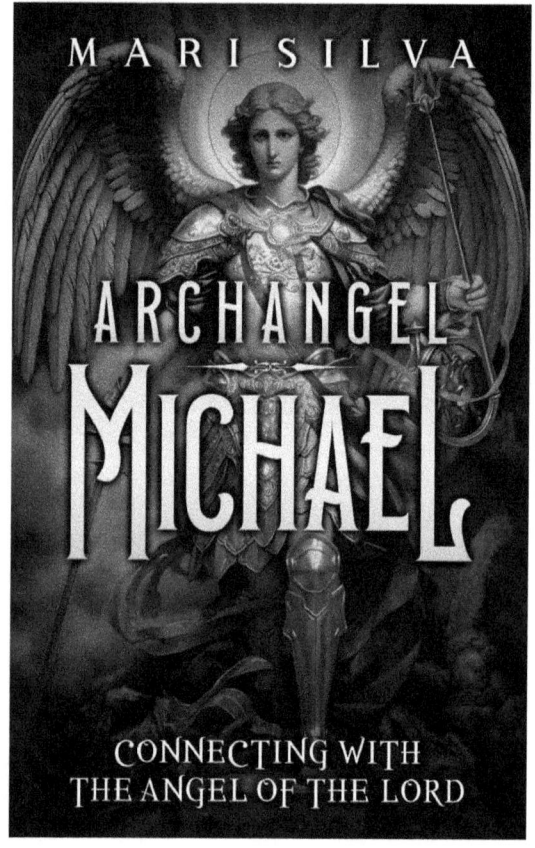

Your Free Gift
(only available for a limited time)

Thanks for getting this book! If you want to learn more about various spirituality topics, then join Mari Silva's community and get a free guided meditation MP3 for awakening your third eye. This guided meditation mp3 is designed to open and strengthen ones third eye so you can experience a higher state of consciousness. Simply visit the link below the image to get started.

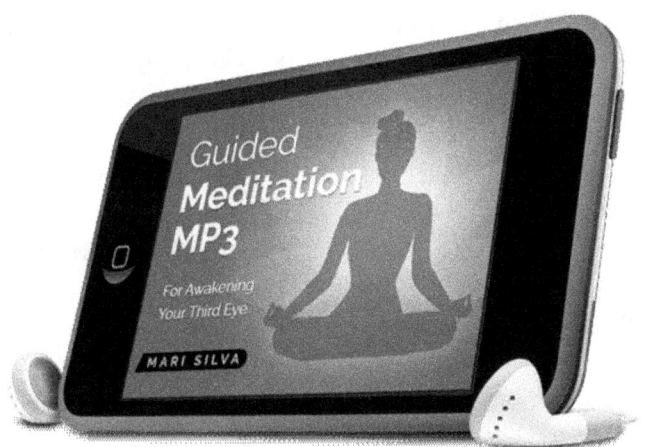

https://spiritualityspot.com/meditation

References

Barker, M. (2006). The Angel Raphael in the Book of Tobit. In M. Bredin (Ed.), Studies in the Book of Tobit. A&C Black.

Barnes, W. H. (1993). Archangels. In M. D. Coogan & B. M. Metzger (Eds.), The Oxford Companion to the Bible. Oxford University Press.

Coogan, M. D. (1993). Raphael. In M. D. Coogan & B. M. Metzger (Eds.), The Oxford Companion to the Bible. Oxford University Press.

Cresswell, J. (2011). Archangels. In J. Cresswell (Ed.), The Watkins Dictionary of Angels. Duncan Baird Publishers.

Cyr, M. D. (1987). The Archangel Raphael: Narrative Authority in Milton's War in Heaven. The Journal of Narrative Technique.

Esler, P. F. (2017). God's Court and Courtiers in the Book of the Watchers. Wipf and Stock Publishers.

Grabbe, L. (2003). Tobit. In J.D.G Dunn (Ed.), Eerdmans Commentary on the Bible. Eerdmans.

Grossman, M.L. (2011). Angels. In M.L Grossman (Ed.), The Oxford Dictionary of the Jewish Religion. Oxford University Press.

Laptas, M. (2016). Archangel Raphael as protector, demon tamer, guide, and healer. Some aspects of the Archangel's activities in Nubian painting. In Aegyptus et Nubia Christiana. The Wlodzimierz Godlewski jubilee volume on the occasion of his 70th birthday. Wydawnictwa Uniwersytetu Warszawskiego.

Lasota, M. (2003). Archangel Raphael. iUniverse.

LaSota, M., & Sternberg, H. (2007). Hope, help, healing with archangel Raphael and the angels. iUniverse.

Mach, M.(1999). Raphael.In K.Van der Toorn,B.Becking,& P.W.Van der

Horst(Eds.), Dictionary of Deities and Demons in the Bible. Eerdmans.

Meier,S.A.(1999).Angel I.In K.Van der Toorn,B.Becking,& P.W.Van der Horst(Eds.), Dictionary of Deities and Demons in the Bible. Eerdmans.

Schaller,B.(1999).Enoch.In G.W.Bromiley(Ed.),The Encyclopedia of Christianity(Vol 2), Eerdmans.

Soll,W.(2000).Raphael.In D.N.Freedman&A.C.Myers(Eds.), Eerdmans Dictionary of the Bible. Eerdmans.

Van Henten,J.W.(1999).Archangel.In K.Van der Toorn,B.Becking,& P.W.Van der Horst(Eds.), Dictionary of Deities and Demons in the Bible. Eerdmans.

Virtue, D. (2011). Archangels 101: How to Connect Closely with Archangels Michael, Raphael, Gabriel, Uriel, and Others for Healing, Protection, and Guidance. Hay House Incorporated.

Virtue, D. (2010). The Healing Miracles of Archangel Raphael. Hay House, Inc.

Webster, R. (2012). Raphael: Communicating with the Archangel for Healing & Creativity. Llewellyn Worldwide

www.ingramcontent.com/pod-product-compliance
Lightning Source LLC
Chambersburg PA
CBHW051843160426
43209CB00006B/1142